Ian Williams was born in Trinidad and raised in Brampton, Canada. In 2019, he won Canada's most prestigious literary award, the Scotiabank Giller Prize, for his debut novel, *Reproduction*. His poetry collection, *Personals*, was short-listed for the Griffin Poetry Prize and the Robert Kroetsch Poetry Book Award. His short story collection, *Not Anyone's Anything*, won the Danuta Gleed Literary Award for the best first collection of short fiction in Canada. His third poetry collection, *Word Problems*, recently won the Raymond Souster Award. He lives in Toronto.

www.ianwilliams.ca • @ianwillwrite

ALSO BY

IAN WILLIAMS

Reproduction

DISORIENTATION

Ian Williams

DISORIENTATION

BEING BLACK IN THE WORLD

Europa
editions

Europa Editions
1 Penn Plaza, Suite 6282
New York, N.Y. 10019
www.europaeditions.com
info@europaeditions.com

Library of Congress Cataloging in Publication Data is available
ISBN 978-1-60945-739-6

Williams, Ian
Disorientation

Book design by Emanuele Ragnisco
www.mekkanografici.com

Original jacket design: Lisa Jager
Image credits: TK

Prepress by Grafica Punto Print – Rome

Printed in the USA

CONTENTS

For my father
who will likely agree

and for Phanuel
who is free to disagree

DISORIENTATION

PART 1

More Than Half of Americans Can't Swim

I have come to believe over and over again that what is most important to me must be spoken, made verbal and shared, even at the risk of having it bruised or misunderstood.
—Audre Lorde

Swimming

My resolution this year is to learn how to swim. It was my resolution last year. And the year before. And, well, let's stop there. I imagine myself falling out of a burning airplane into the ocean like an action hero. I crash into the water, conscious for a hopeful moment, before floundering and drowning. The scenario is illogical, but I have my reasons.

I also have several reasons for why it is taking me so long to learn.

1. All the pools that I've entered have been unpleasantly cold and I don't like the sensation of cold water on my body, especially my back. I don't like the sound of underwater in my ears. You can feel the current of conversations around race, particularly in America. You're entering an environment that has cast you as rebellious, violent, and troublemaking, if Black, and as blameworthy, racist, and heartless, if white. None of this feels good washing over your head.
2. I haven't learned how to swim because of a story, internalized from childhood, that my aunt told of a

Black boy in England who was struggling in a pool. He could have drowned. And the swimming instructor said, *Leave him. N███ don't float anyhow.* I imagine the instructor turning away to deal with the white students while the Black child splashed and gulped. You already have an internal story that makes you reluctant or fearful to approach the subject of race. If you're Black, you expect any attempt to be met with pity or demands for proof. You've learned early that any mention of a white person in a racial situation that affects you is akin to an accusation. So you bear the microaggressions. If white, maybe you witnessed another white person get eviscerated for a joke or watching out for the welfare of the neighbourhood. So you're just going to avoid Black people. If you see one leaning against a car, you're not going to call the police (that's probably for the best). You're not going to say *anything whatsoever* about race, because you're not stupid.

3. The thought of learning to swim among six-year-olds with water wings could be an amusing future anecdote, but I'd rather not endure the present awkwardness. I should know how to swim by now. So pride gets in the way. This type of pride is buoyed by shame rather than deflated by it. You should know more about race, but you're embarrassed to be counted among the ignorant, so you don't ask. Of course, there are adult swimming classes. My racialized friend attended the first session of one where the entire class comprised three shirtless racialized men. It was like

Swimming for Immigrants, he said. You don't want to be in the company of people like you.

4. Let's say I survive the classes and learn how to swim. Once the lessons are over, where will I go swimming? Am I going to doggy-paddle in some public pool with Olympians zooming and sharking around me? Who's eager to get into emotionally murky waters with people who've been swimming a long time?

5. I'm afraid of the deep end. I wouldn't mind staying in the shallow end where I could put my feet down. Maybe I just need to learn how to float. If the plane crashes and I survive the impact, I could float on the water until help comes. When I got tired, I'd hold on to buoyant debris, like Kate Winslet in *Titanic*. You can keep your head above water with a few popular opinions. You don't need to look into the faces of slaves in photographs. You get it. *Slavery bad, equality good. Respect Black people.*

If you're Black, you believe that your experience excuses you from understanding exactly what happened back then. You're Black and that's enough. This one's tricky. Your experience is important, yes, but it's not everything. When you position yourself in history, you enter into a community of people with similar experiences and you observe how the racial climate changes over time. For white people, it's worth learning some history and theory and more: it's worth having experiences of disorientation and discomfort, as a means of empathy and as a way of accessing courage, which only grows from challenge and exercise.

6. I have a sensitive bladder. I am concerned that in a moment of stress I might piss in the pool and get banned forever. For starters, don't piss in the pool. There are places for that. Don't contaminate discussions by trolling around and advocating on behalf of the devil. Not pissing in the pool is for your own good too. There are Internet forums full of piss. I doubt you want to swim in the putrid opinions of narrow-minded folks. If that's what you want, you probably shouldn't be swimming. You probably should find a community of kinky people and have them piss on you.

Although I've wanted to swim for an embarrassingly long time, I have no ambitions to be a lifeguard. In fact, if you told me that I should learn to swim so that I could save other people, I'd say, Great, but what's in it for me? So much for the kindness of my heart. Of course, you're more likely to leave comfortable ignorance behind if there is a benefit to you and not just a benefit to other people. What does that say about you, though?

Our benefits are inextricable. It's benefit enough that I can be with you on land or water. No saving needs to happen. In water, we each look a little different because we're both affected by the same element. The journey out of ignorance takes us into—forgive the mushy term— self-discovery and into a deeper empathetic relation to the prevailing issues of our time.

* * *

I don't know where the scenario of my plunging into the ocean and needing to swim to safety came from.

It is estimated that at least two million Black people died while crossing the Atlantic Ocean on slave ships. Some jumped, choosing to drown rather than to be enslaved.

A POLITICAL PERSON

I do not consider myself a political person in any sense of the word. I turn away from CNN maps on election night. I care about race, but I don't march in the streets with homemade signs. I've been to one protest, out of curiosity more than conviction. In truth, I care too much about the subject to see it batted between acquaintances as only a subject of conversation.

Despite this apolitical stance, offensive especially to people who view all politics as inescapable, I've known which opinions to hold, how to shade them depending on the company around me. I haven't always believed these opinions, I've accepted them. Accepting conflict and conflicting perspectives seems a precondition for getting political.

How does one engage with the explosive world of race and privilege?

As a Black man, I could claim expertise. Race is one of the few places where white people actually defer to Black people without challenge. White people think race lives in Black bodies. They don't see whiteness as having meaningful contributions to make to racial conversations. The belief that race lives only in certain bodies is a powerful acknowledgement that the structures we live in are racist. Knowing this dynamic (and hesitant to take on the extra work of carrying race for white people), I've protected my little life for the most part, though I sometimes subject my experiences to the glare of theory and terms, to the words *microaggression* and *anti-racist*. I categorize my experiences, but then I open my arms and they come waddling back to me, shedding labels, dishevelled and unruly. I am not the Blaxpert. By renouncing expertise, I am not turning my experience over to other people. Blackness is not for white anthropologists or diversity trainers to determine.

And why do you need an expert? Why do you need a race guru? You have a mirror. Why do you look at a photo of a cover model to make sense of your own face?

I know a fair bit, but never enough to seize authority. My dissatisfaction with my knowledge, coupled with my tepid emotions, occasionally nauseates me. Would I not be a better human if I were informed and angry? Then I could be righteous. I should be vocal. More than vocal. Loud. I have received the message that to be Black these days is to be perpetually outraged and distressed, fed up, tired. To be anything apart from that is treacherous and out of touch.

If you're like me, you resist people who pressure you to see the world as they do, to care about what they do, to prioritize what they prioritize. I see that as a kind of interpersonal fascism. What they believe, care about, prioritize, might well be important, in which case I will make my way to that side; my resistance is less to the truth of what they say than to their methods of force, shame, mandatory acceptance. Stop behaving like bad religious proselytizers. Chill. I'll decide when I have the info, not on your schedule, not on your terms, not even if you believe everything is political. Grand, absolute statements are also totalitarian.

SILENCE

Take, for example, this Instagram post that a friend forwarded to me.

The post is a multi-part polemic that lambastes the passive, cat-clicking social media user: "Fear of 'getting political' on your social media is, at its core, racist." A little later, the point gets reiterated as an equation: "To sit in silence is to let people die."

This post was liked by 416,267 people, but the comments

were mostly negative: "This is a pile of bollocks if ever I've read any"; "bro, then im racist af."

When you see Instagram posts like this, you find yourself implicated in a noisy political landscape. So where's your statement? Huh? What are your politics? What is your plan for action? Where will you post it? Are you angry at something? Have you found someone to hate?

In a culture that demands statements from corporations and pressures individuals to lay their politics bare on inhospitable platforms, many of us have had to rethink how we translate our personal, inarticulate convictions for public inspection. These public declarations are difficult for people who are inclined to privacy and even more complicated if you're Black. As a Black person, one grows wary of the discrepancy between what people claim to believe and how they actually respond to one's existence. By the time you reach middle age, quite battered by the accumulation of false claims, you find it hard to trust and forgive, to accept a hopeful prognosis because of a promise.

When the Instagram post elsewhere declares, "A refusal to post is, at its core, a refusal to give up your comfort. A refusal to give up your power as a privileged individual," I realize as usual that this post is not meant for me. It suggests that privilege keeps one calm, not the years spent developing composure under a discriminatory system. It fails to see how, for many Black people, the time that the world is prepared to listen does not coincide with the time that we wanted to speak. You can listen to remixes of our equity movements from the 1860s, the 1950s, the 1960s—from any decade to the present. The recent statements, militant in tone, decontextualized by virtue of their platforms, give the impression of being revolutionary. They draw up lists of alliances and enemies. Tell me whether you agree with me or not. Agree with me or else.

I am troubled by the extremity of rhetoric, not just in this post but in the discourse around race in general. Eurocentric→white supremacist. Microaggression→racial abuse. Silence→complicity. Or in the words of the Original Poster's equation: "To sit in silence is to let people die." Extreme.

I do not post a comment. I do not share the story.

I think about race a lot—every day, several times a day. But that internal activity rarely gets externalized. Sure, there's the fear that I'll say the wrong thing, meaning in my case that I'll repeat some uninterrogated white ideology and a sister with big Africa earrings will call me the white man's whip. Or I'll say something about racist institutions and hurt the white people who do nothing but lend me books. Race is not easy to talk about.

Once, I was so frustrated that I screamed in my car while speeding along the highway. But I can't go around screaming to express myself.

On the other extreme, as I mentioned before, I don't want to position myself as an expert where I open my palm and up pops a hologram of a plantation like in a sci-fi movie so I can explain it from all angles, then systematically present intellectual arguments to pummel white people into shame. I've seen people do it. That's more of a performance than a conversation. Black people in the audience shout,

"Preach," and white people leave the auditorium satisfactorily flagellated. Being on either side of chastisement doesn't appeal to me at all.

Neither do I want to perform vulnerability or prove that I am human by supplying countless anecdotes of the racial injuries I have sustained. Here is a lifetime of hurt, grant me membership into humankind. Make me one of you. That's not the level of conversation I'd like to have in this century. A contemporary exchange should be premised on the understanding that Black humans are wired like all humans to bruise from injustice, from affronts to our dignity, our good intentions, our reputation.

As a fourth option, I could talk about race like a comic does. Employing a defence mechanism against injury, I'd turn everything into a joke. A funny thing happened to me the other day. Can you believe that white guy? But I am not the butt of a joke.

For white people, your entrance to conversations on race is likewise restricted. Your speaking position is predetermined as racist or woke or well-meaning or clueless or nervous or ignorant. Given the options for Black and white people alike, we often opt for silence. Because the subject matter is already scripted and directed for me, I find myself disapproving of how I will say what I have not yet said.

The question returns: How does one engage with the explosive world of race and privilege? I started writing this book because I wanted to get all of my ideas down in one place. I was talking to myself, and the simmering, disorganized mess internally was not much different from the mess in the world, though without the cruelty.

I have made a contract with myself to speak the truth, to speak only as myself, and to take the risk of speaking.

If I limit myself to saying only the things I believe are true, then I enter conversations with an ethical commitment to truth. This way my convictions will be tested before I share them and I will leave conversations with my integrity intact. If I am unsure, if I am underinformed, or ignorant, I will admit it. The common alternative to speaking examined truths is regurgitating received, broken-telephone-game ideas about race.

Speaking as myself means speaking out of my experience and knowledge. Both of these are expandable, one with openness, the other with effort. I cannot reasonably be called on to represent the wide range of Black experience, which is not to say that I will neglect the concerns of people who are being overlooked. As far as possible, I'd prefer to make direct links between the people asking and the people with answers. Incarcerated men are available for comment on the system that incarcerated them. Why don't people ask them? Speaking as myself also means that I will use my own vocabulary and my comfortable emotional registers. I'm not an opera singer.

The third part of my contract, taking risks, makes me more courageous to enter a war against tyranny. I'm framing it as a war so that I can find for myself what is worth fighting for. The long, arbitrary subjugation of one group of people so that other people could shore up privilege is worth having some thoughts on. I accept that people will misinterpret or disagree with my positions. These disagreements ought to test and tune my own thinking, rather than make me defensive and inhospitable. Thinking around race needs to be elastic and responsive, because racism travels faster than our ability to predict or detect it.

Here's a kind of risky thing to say because it's unformed and could so easily be misinterpreted. Imagine if we all had, as with a sexual orientation, a racial orientation. I don't mean an attraction to a certain race; I mean something more like a racial awareness/orientation that unfolds and finds expression over time. It would mean white folks don't get to be normative and invisible. In another meaning, *orientation* would suggest an exposure to the history of race and the ways it continues to operate. It also invokes the fact that we have all been oriented or socialized toward a preferred race, whiteness, whether we are white or not. It's a bit silly, I know, I know. But I would like to explore that kind of thing outside my head without a guillotine hovering.

BEING WRONG

The guillotine these days is for people who have the "wrong" truth, who cause offence when speaking as themselves, and who take a risk in breaking silence. Anyone, really.

Consider David Foster Wallace. If he were alive today, his head would be in a basket. I like this scenario from "Authority and American Usage," an essay he wrote about the dictionary, because some people would see his interaction with a Black student as a virtuosic model and others as a train wreck. Wallace is speaking in his role as a professor.

We think of professors as enlightened and of universities as progressive spaces. Here we have an intelligent, ethically rigorous white man who was nonetheless imperfect. With respect to race and Black interiority, he was ignorant at best or dismissive at worst.

Good Cop David sits down "certain black students who were (a) bright and inquisitive as hell and (b) deficient in what US higher education considers written English facility." Bad Cop Wallace enters: "let me spell something out in my official teacher-voice." He asks the Black student a patronizing question that cuts to the heart of ignorance: "How much of this stuff do you already know?" He portrays the student as fluent in Standard Black English but ignorant that SWE is required of her. By SWE, he means Standard Written English, but he admits it could just as easily be called Standard White English.

Good Cop David commiserates that other profs "won't let you write in SBE. Maybe it seems unfair." He sets himself up as the alternative. Then, whammo, Bad Cop returns: "I'm not going to let you write in SBE either. In my class, you have to learn and write in SWE." And again, the emphasis falls on his power: "In class—in my English class—you will have to master and write in Standard Written English," and here comes the full force of whiteness aware of itself, "which we might just as well call 'Standard White English' because it was developed by white people and is used by white people, especially educated, powerful white people."

At this point, I imagine the Black student is totally disoriented by the white-supremacist turn in the conversation.

Should she resist his reasoning? Can one report star professor David Foster Wallace? To whom? Is it even possible to get an A in this course anymore, knowing that this man has marked her as delinquent? Has the withdrawal deadline passed? Will it be dark outside when she leaves his office, and what's the best-lit route to her dorm?

Suddenly, Good Cop David is back: "I'm respecting you enough here to give you what I believe is the straight truth."

Then Bad Cop Wallace pulls on his white hood: "In this country, SWE is perceived as the dialect of education and intelligence and power and prestige, and anybody of any race, ethnicity, religion, or gender who wants to succeed in American culture has got to be able to use SWE. This is just How It Is."

Bad Cop Wallace goes on to pre-empt her reactions. If the Black student is pissed or thinks the system is racist, she can spend her whole life fighting against his convictions, but those arguments will have to be made in SWE "because SWE is the dialect our nation uses to talk to itself."

I will the Black student to lower her eyebrows and reposition her dropped jaw. Wallace is telling her that she can't do jack about conformity to whiteness, and that "African Americans who've become successful and important in US culture know this." Audre Lorde is willing the Black student to quote her: "The master's tools will never dismantle the master's house."

And here's good cop and bad cop merged into one final chokehold: "And [STUDENT'S NAME] you're going to learn to use it, too, because I am going to make you."

Students were offended by his position, and one did file an official complaint. Colleagues told him that he was "racially insensitive." He responded that "the cultural and political realities of American life are themselves racially insensitive and elitist and offensive and unfair." Wallace has a point, of course. But what seems to be missing here is the awareness that his version of straight talk only amplifies and replicates systemic offences while the work of dismantling them continues to belong to the Black student, whose powerlessness he has repeatedly established.

Wallace presents a formidable argument for conformity. I think even a young James Baldwin or Audre Lorde, despite their potential, would find it challenging to respond in the moment. If young Lorde were sitting across from him, she could say, "Survival is not an academic skill." She could say, "Difference must not be merely tolerated, but seen as a fund of necessary polarities between which our creativity can spark like a dialectic." In other words, between SBE and SWE is a conversation about power. Why must the work fall on the Black student to close the breach between groups? Black people are tired of doing the work to undo racism, which is not a problem we created. Would it be any more work to appreciate SBE than it would be to appreciate Black music? But the fear of contamination keeps white people from engaging with Black expression until it becomes profitable economically or culturally.

I'd like to believe that if David Foster Wallace were alive today and paying attention to the current racial conversations in America, he'd have a significantly revised version of this speech. That it would have become a conversation, not a speech. Instead of expecting the student to step toward whiteness, he would step toward Blackness. I see in him, not here specifically but over the course of his work, the potential of white people to become less casual about the psychic violence they do to Black people. I know he's dead and I know there's no way to confirm his trajectory. Yet the evidence of his thoughtfulness and humility indicates a white man with capacity for growth. His curiosity and self-analysis prevent him from being wilfully ignorant. Can we forgive a person their ignorance? Can we take heart that dead white people might yet change their minds?

POSITIONS

More questions coming your way. Where do you stand on debates about Standard English, affirmative action, reparations? Should white people lead civil rights movements? Should they teach Black studies? Should we even use the term Black? Do we pursue justice peacefully or by any means necessary?

There's no consensus among Black folk. Are you ready for this fact? Black people disagree with each other. Sometimes disagreements get ugly. Marcus Garvey and W.E.B. Du Bois's disagreements over Pan-Africanism degenerated into personal attacks. Du Bois, usually dignified and refined, called Garvey a "little, fat, black man; ugly." Garvey clapped back with, "It is no wonder that DuBois seeks the company of white people, because he hates black as being ugly. That is why he likes to dance with white people, and dine with them, and sometimes sleep with them." Du Bois responds: "Marcus Garvey is, without doubt, the most dangerous enemy of the Negro race in America and in the world. He is either a lunatic or a traitor."

Black-on-Black disagreement gets portrayed as degeneracy, but it is simply a consequence of free thought. Ideally, in cases where we disagree with others, we practise tolerance. Not the patronizing kind. True tolerance allows us to pause on other people's opinions, to regard them as valid to their espousers, without embracing or dismissing them.

Moreover, one person can make compelling, conflicting arguments over a lifetime. Take the question of violence, for example. We like to believe Martin Luther King was born a pacifist, but at one point he actually believed that "war, horrible as it is, might be preferable to surrender to a totalitarian system—Nazi, Fascist, or Communist." King's position evolved over time to the point where he believed "nonviolence offers the only road to freedom for my people." He was not born with a fully formed moral intelligence: "Like most people, I had heard of Gandhi, but I had never studied him seriously." Even the great Martin Luther King had to start somewhere: he bought a "half-dozen books on Gandhi's life and works."

My point here is not to tell you what position to hold but to suggest that positions are not fixed territory to defend forever. If you clicked Like on a post three years ago because the headline seemed logical, you are not required to stand by that tiny muscle spasm until death. Positions change as the context around them widens. Our moment unfortunately requires contextual coherence to the point of demanding consistency of character from everyone. As a society, we have been expecting more and more contextual knowledge from each other. Don't use *minority* because it diminishes *people of colour*. The statue in our neighbourhood, do you know what that guy did?

Because we can't realistically know everything, humility is the best companion to ignorance.

My mother's oldest friend from childhood lost her son in the ocean. A few months after getting married, the son went on vacation with his wife. She went out for a swim and was pulled far out from shore. He jumped in to save her. They both vanished from sight. Her body washed up later that day and his was discovered the following morning.

They both knew how to swim, yet they both drowned.

Until the final few drafts, this essay was called "Ignorance" because I thought knowledge could save us from drowning. But all the knowledge in the world seems to be no match for the current, the rough water in which we find ourselves. I think ignorance is adjacent to a bigger problem, the problem of the self and its corollaries. Selfishness, self-centredness, self-protection. Black people care about race because it affects us. White people don't care about race until it affects them. Hope lies in caring for something beyond the self.

The man in the ocean knew how to swim and he drowned. But he died in love with his wife, opting to go down with her rather than stand on the shore in safety. Even when he was in the ocean, there must have been a point when he could have turned back and saved himself. I imagine his hand in those last moments above the surface, grasping air.

Or maybe he found what he went searching for. He reached his wife. Maybe he died with his wife in his arms.

DISORIENTATION

*So you're waiting, even if you don't quite know it, wait-
ing for the moment when you realise that you really are
different to them; that there are people out there, like
Madame, who don't hate you or wish you any harm, but
who nevertheless shudder at the very thought of you—
of how you were brought into this world and why—and
who dread the idea of your hand brushing against theirs.*
—KAZUO ISHIGURO, *Never Let Me Go*

1. DISORIENTING FAMILY

My brother married a white woman. My family is not
sure how this came to pass, seeing as all his girlfriends to
that point, as far as we knew, had been Black. As a
teenager, he was adamant about going to a Black high
school (Central Peel, nicknamed Central Africa). He listened to Big Daddy Kane, Nas, and Biggie Smalls on his
Walkman so our mother couldn't hear the swearing. He
played basketball behind a Catholic school. He watched
Fresh Prince and Spike Lee's *Malcolm X*. He wore his
clothes baggy. His jeans sagged down his skinny butt. He
kept his sneakers spotless with a toothbrush. Got a fade
every two weeks at the cool barbershop, not the one for old
men. He was casual about school, dropped courses, failed
math once, took only what was essential to get into university. When the time came to apply and our mother pressed
him to try for York University in Toronto, my brother laid
down the ultimatum that he was going to a Black college in
America or no college at all. All of which is to say that he

was a textbook of Black suburban adolescence, with proper ratios of swagger and resistance. So the family was perplexed when he called us a couple of years into his working life to say that he was getting married to a white woman from Alabama.

Time passed. My brother and his wife had a daughter. They bought a house. They sold it. They relocated from Alabama to North Carolina, just outside Charlotte. They bought another house. They had a son.

Now you're caught up.

One morning, my brother was driving his daughter to school. It was clear, as they drew near, that she had something on her mind. She told him that the day before, a girl had called her a n████. What did the word signal about her? Why would this girl call her that? What should she do? The moment in childhood when one realizes that one is Black is profoundly disorienting. Internally, my niece had been knocked off balance and wanted her dad to tell her whether the limp would be permanent.

You're hanging out in a hallway with a group of girls during recess. A few of you don't have a phone, so you take turns passing around the phone of a rat-faced girl. No one really likes her, but she's grown-up in a way that you all envy. And she has a phone. At the moment, you have hold of it, but she wants her phone back. You shoulder her so you can keep scrolling through video suggestions of dance routines. The other girls huddle around you, and the rat-faced girl, growing desperate to be at the centre, says, You're such a n████.

Now, your main pursuit for the last few minutes has been finding the best dance video for all the girls to imitate, but this new element makes everyone look up from the screen to the impending confrontation between you and this girl. The girl has somehow managed to dethrone you with that word. Her word, everyone seems to know, trumps *rat face*, which you've called her behind her back. You're ten. What is happening? What does Ratface have over you suddenly? How can you rally the other girls again? Why wasn't Becky a n▪▪▪▪ when she pushed Ratface down?

You search for the difference between you and everyone else. You know all about differences. You bully and are bullied based on the differences between boy and girl, fat and thin, sickly and strong. You know about Black and white. But what's new is that it has been singled out with such powerful, historical irrefutability. This has to have something to do with your dreadlocked father who drops you off. You are also aware that the rest of your concerns haven't been diminished by the appearance of this new one. The bell will go and after recess you will have to convert an endless number of fractions to decimals. The day was supposed to be forgettable. Should you tell someone? You return to the sensation of the phone still in your hand. The sounds of children's voices reach you. Uniformed bodies storm the hallway.

* * *

Disorientation refers to the effect of racial encounters on racialized people, the whiplash of race that occurs while minding one's business.

It reminds you of your race, usually at a moment when your internal experience is not framed in racial terms, and reorders the pattern of your interactions around race.

It disrupts your reality. It is enacted on you—it interrupts. It stalls the forward momentum of your life. You can't prepare for disorientation. Try walking around in an armoured suit.

Disorientation suggests to you that you are in the wrong time and place. When's the wrong time? Now. A time warp deposits you in the past. Where's the wrong place? Your car, a public park, coffee shops, the sidewalk, an elevator, your bed.

Sometimes the consequences are irritating. Sometimes they are deadly.

2. DISORIENTING CHILDHOOD

A quick survey of my bookshelf reveals that most Black autobiographical narratives describe a moment of disorientation. The Black epiphany, if you will, becomes linked to a moment of formative racialization.

- The beginning of racialization for Venture Smith, author of one of the earliest slave narratives, comes as a literal ambush. A "violent blow on the head." A rope around his neck. A march toward the sea.
- In 1757, writer Olaudah Equiano beholds a slave ship and white people for the first time. He is so disoriented that he thinks he has entered a spiritual dimension: "I

was now persuaded that I had gotten into a world of bad spirits, and that they were going to kill me." His words for disorientation are *astonishment* and *terror*, feelings that later settle into *horror* and *anguish*. His disorientation at seeing Black people chained together on the ship, at seeing the system of whiteness at work, is so overpowering that he faints "motionless on the deck."

- As a little boy in nineteenth-century New England, W.E.B. Du Bois is disoriented when a tall white girl rejects his calling card: "Then it dawned upon me with a certain suddenness that I was different from the others; or like, mayhap, in heart and life and longing, but shut out from their world by a vast veil." For Du Bois, that moment of disorientation is sudden, clarifying, a "revelation [that] first burst upon one, all in a day."

- James Baldwin realizes at the age of five or six that "the flag to which you have pledged allegiance, along with everybody else, has not pledged allegiance to you." Describing that "great shock" in a speech later in life, he argues that we enter the world with a sense of equality until a moment or period of disorientation intervenes.

- In West Baltimore, in 1986, a kid pulls a gun on Ta-Nehisi Coates. He goes home and realizes that other kids, those on TV, those in the suburbs, do not fear for their bodies. "I felt, but did not yet understand, the relation between that other world and me." His epiphany is of "a cosmic injustice, a profound cruelty."

- In third grade, around the end of the 1980s, Ibram X. Kendi comes to understand that injustice or unfairness is not, in fact, arbitrary. He notices his white teacher ignore the hand of a shy Black girl, who has worked up the courage to participate, only to call on a favoured white student. He recalls his fury and her sadness. From the back of the class, to recover, he says, "I needed some time to think."

- In *How to Be Black*, Baratunde Thurston surveys his friends to find out when they realized they were Black and what Blackness meant, an experiment I don't need to repeat. One woman, Jacquetta Szathmari, recalls that one day at day camp, as she was about to dive into the water, a white kid said that the grease in her hair would ruin Chesapeake Bay. You can hear how stunned she was in the moment: "I was like, 'Wow, okay, that's racism, and that's what it's going to mean for a little while for me to be black.'" More pointedly: "That's when I realized that maybe being black could suck a little bit."

- The present. A girl calls my niece a n███.

My niece had heard the word n███ before in the very car where she told my brother about the incident. My brother enjoys his music. The word is integral to rap. It's used in many ways. His daughter had asked about it. Why they keep saying that? My brother, I imagine, unwilling to give up his music to the erosion of middle age, taught her about context—who says n███ and, somewhat confusingly, why she shouldn't.

My brother and I knew the word *n███* before it was ever used on us. (Because of his children, I won't tell you how it was used on him.) In Trinidad, where we were born, children make choices by singing:

> Eeenie, meenie, minie, mo.
> Catch a n████ by the toe.
> When he ready, let him go.
> Eenie, meenie, minie, mo.

In Canada, kids sang a sanitized version involving a tiger. When we first heard it, my brother and I looked at each other, surprised by their naïveté.

In all of the above cases of disorientation, differences are amplified.

In all cases, the disorientation that accompanies racial experiences marks an emerging awareness of white dominance, and a place for the Black person in the hierarchy of whiteness.

In all cases, this awareness comes suddenly, at a time when one is unprepared to think of oneself in racial terms.

In all cases, disorientation is the reaction to a somewhat violent action. It's the violence of being born. Racialized people are born again into a system we do not choose to inherit. But, inevitably, we must be born.

No doubt, children often have an understanding of difference and race before a direct encounter with it. These moments of disorientation are not simply the introduction of a concept, but recruit people into participating in the ordering system of whiteness, with or without their consent. Whether these experiences are, in fact, the first or the fiftieth incident is not important. The important thing is how significant such a childhood experience can be for restructuring a person's understanding of the world.

White kids don't have those racially disorienting moments, at least not in the same way. If they are mocked for freckles or red hair or a piggish nose, it's not racialized. It comes with an understanding of a rather benign difference amplified, but without systemic backing.

For Black children, early moments of disorientation are rarely linked to, *Oh, what lovely braids you have.* Race is rarely introduced in a framework that is positive, affirmative, empowering, almost never superior—unless by one's parents.

For Du Bois and Kendi, disorientation came as refusals to be acknowledged. For Smith, Equiano, and Coates, it came from being in sudden physical danger. For my niece, it came verbally at school when she was called n█████. For a lot of us, our first hierarchical introduction to race, our "blow on the head," is linked to that word. I'm going to say it and only this once. *Nigger.*

3. N█████

I have no way of conducting this study, but I suspect that most Black people have been called n█████ at some point in their lives.

Most recently, in Colorado, I was called a n█████ by a homeless Indigenous man because I didn't give him money. I remember the 7-Eleven clearly, the corner, the direction I was walking, like the scene of an accident.

Years before, I went to a conference in San Antonio. There must have been a biker convention in town at the same time because I saw many large white men wearing altogether too much black leather in the lobby. After checking in, I entered an elevator with two such men. The doors closed and they continued a story about something, I don't remember what. I only remember that n███ was thrown around altogether too much by one man. The other man's job was mostly to snicker. They were at the back. I was facing the door with my luggage, counting the floors. It couldn't have been a long time. At my floor, the doors opened and I got out. They continued their ascent.

On that same trip to San Antonio, when I was walking from my hotel to the conference venue, a similar thing happened. Behind me were two men, again talking about some n███ that I hoped wasn't me. No matter how I adjusted my gait, they seemed neither to speed up and pass nor to drop back and fall out of earshot. I remember there was a chain fence on my left, like for construction, and traffic on my right, and of course the men behind me. The only way I could escape was by moving forward. I definitely couldn't even look back to acknowledge them or to investigate. I think I turned a corner as soon as I could, taking myself off route. I remember the feeling—as if I was suddenly in a dream—of being pursued by two men and the word n███, which was not intended for me any more than a stray bullet is intended for its victim.

Now, on the surface, it seems like nothing big happened in San Antonio. If I told this story to a white friend, they'd acknowledge it, then brush it away with, *What a bunch of racist idiots*, and that would be that. *They weren't speaking to you.* But my Black friends can extract from these incidents degrees of violence—that the words were intended to be overheard by me, that I was no match for the two men if I dared protest, that the men in the elevator had seen me punch in my floor number and turn in the direction of my room. Black people know that in a strange town where you need to buy meals and move around alone, you begin to question your right to take up space, that your vigilance increases, that you should probably call someone back home and tell them what happened, just in case. And they understand too that you have a conference paper to give the next day in a room where you're likely to be the only Black person. Your obligations to the world don't stop despite its hostility to you.

James Baldwin writes about an experience in a Swiss village, where children shout *Neger! Neger!* at him as he walks down the street. Again, disorientation for him registers as shock: "It must be admitted that in the beginning I was far too shocked to have any real reaction." In the wake, he tries to be pleasant, posits excuses for the children, blames their ignorance, their curiosity, bleaches their motives. His benevolence to these children does not stop despite the pain they cause him.

While my instincts tell me that most Black people have these kinds of verbally violent experiences, I want to know how many white people have used the word. And how. Did they call someone a n▮▮▮ while in a city, out of earshot from their home? In the car while driving? At home, after a long day?

I'm extrapolating backward from the girl who called my niece a n█████ to the household where she learned the word. I doubt she came from a family of KKK Grand Wizards. Maybe the word was thrown around in reference to a client or a colleague while venting the soap opera of the day at dinner. Maybe it was said about a friend's Black boyfriend. The kid picked it up when her parents didn't think she was listening. She also picked up how to leverage the word for one's power and another person's humiliation.

Here. I'll put my story next to my niece's. I had buried this memory. I unwillingly went with my brother to play basketball at a school gym one evening. It was a package deal with our parents: he could go if he took me along. My brother quickly found his friends and played half-court. I got a ball and was shooting alone, bored. I'm really no good at basketball. My errant ball interrupted a couple of kids who were playing one-on-one, and one of those kids called me a n█████. There. I was in middle school at the time. I don't remember much else, except feeling like a loser who had a cool older brother and no friends of his own.

4. Disorienting Adulthood

Of course, disorientation isn't limited to the word n█████, neither is it restricted to childhood. For Black people, disorientation persists beyond an initial epiphany.

Baldwin notes its progress over time: "The disaffection, the demoralization, and the gap between one person and another only on the basis of the color of their skin, begins there [in childhood] and accelerates—accelerates throughout a whole lifetime—to the present when you realize you're thirty and are having a terrible time managing to trust your countrymen." Every racial encounter in the course of one's day is a psychic ambush, the evidence of which, until recently, is collected as accumulated experience rather than an archive of recordings for authentication by evidence seekers.

To re-establish equilibrium after the disorienting effects of racism, Black people develop a variety of strategies, some admittedly defensive. I've found myself evaluating racist incidents on a kind of scale, so I can decide which ones to drop, which to pursue. I sometimes sort anti-Black racism into major aggressions (violence, murder, vandalism), moderate aggressions (traffic stops, suspicious looks, a slur), and microaggressions (jokes, mispronunciations). A moderate event can escalate into a major event; a major event can echo years later as a microaggression. I don't mean these categories prescriptively *at all*, like zones on a fixed trauma scale. I'm just confessing how I've needed to get through some days.

Or I parse incidents somewhat grammatically. Sometimes I am the direct object of an aggression (Colorado) and sometimes I am the indirect object (San Antonio). And sometimes the distance is more distant, such as when I hear reports of racism from others. If, when a friend applies for a mortgage, a bank asks him to supply elaborate records of his finances "to make sure the money's clean," I might classify that as a moderate aggression of which I am the indirect object since it did not happen to me (though, truthfully, something similar did). Then I can consider what kind of action is appropriate. Should one stomach it? Determine whether this is the policy for everyone who applies for a mortgage? Find another lender?

Christina Sharpe writes about anti-Black racism as the weather or climate of our interactions. Whether we are in the rain or watching it through a window, *we are always affected* by racial weather. Learning about the death of a Black man to whom one bears no familial or personal relation can sink weeks of one's life into grief. I was on a Zoom panel around the time of one such murder. It was my birthday. The panel went fine. Actually, if I'm honest, it was painful. After the event, I immediately took off my sweaty shirt and lay on the couch. My partner took a photo of me, from the other side of the birthday flowers, slipping into a grave. Regardless of the magnitude of the event or its intended target or the metaphors we use to contain it, we can't stop such an incident from having a highly disruptive effect on our emotions.

I can no more stop the disorienting effects of such events than I can opt out of weather or grammar. It's not that I find race in everything but that race finds me.

Some racial information comes my way every day. If I go a day without seeing a Black person, I question the city, my circle, my engagement with the world. I eat a piece of chocolate and remember a YouTube video where a Chinese woman asks a Black man, *When you eat chocolate, how do you know where to stop?* I see a white man with a sharp fade—when did that become stylish for them? If someone (white) on the next tennis court only addresses my partner but not me for the hour, I get thrown a little. I'm cleaning my condo for a viewing and wonder if the potential buyers will question the number of books by Black people on my shelves. Will they find one of my curled hairs on the tile and choose not to buy my condo?

Weather blows in from social media. A Brown Muslim brother posts about anti-Black racism in caps. Google tries to be helpful by sending me news notifications. Interracial dating ads pop up in the margin. I'm getting rained on.

Do white people experience racial disorientation?

My agent sent me a blog post by a white woman who got pulled over five times in one year while driving with her poodle. The first time, the officer unbuckled the holster of his gun as he approached her car. He shone his flashlight at her, at the dog, inspected her licence, and notified her that he pulled her over because she was going three miles below the speed limit and was impeding traffic. No ticket. Four times, she was accused of the same violation: impeding traffic. No ticket. Because this kept happening, she got her speedometer checked. It was in working order. The fifth time, she was driving home from her sister's house and a cop trailed her for a mile before pulling her over, although she was careful to obey the speed limit. Two officers approached. The one on the passenger side reached for his gun. They did the usual—took her licence, shone their flashlights around, then told her she was going below the speed limit. The white woman did not get a ticket in any of these cases. Then, while she was having lunch with her father, a former neighbour interrupted the meal to tell her, "There's a Black man stealing your van right now." The pieces clicked. Her poodle. Silhouette. Afro. All the cops thought she had been driving with a Black man.

Since her poodle died, she has not been pulled over once.

Each time it happened, she was disoriented. She described the disorientation as "frustrating." She couldn't make sense of what was happening. Disorientation is emotional: "As a white woman, getting stopped by the police is scary." Disorientation is physical: "It makes my heart race and my stomach hurt. I'm sure a black person's fear and rage is a hundred times greater." Disorientation is mental: "There is the thought, 'What if it's not the real cops?'"

When I last checked, the post had 440 comments, with a smattering of white defensiveness. "This story sounds completely made up." Another poster: "If African American people do not want to be profiled, then clean up your image." Another: "This one person's lived experience is not statistically relevant. Anecdotal evidence may or may not be an outlier." I'll get to evidence in a minute.

So, do white people get racially disoriented? It's not usually a case of mistaking a poodle for a husband. It's a case of racializing them. Calling them white. When they perceive their world slipping or their character being maligned at a time when they don't expect it, they become disoriented. You've heard of the diversity workshop exercise of separating a room by eye colour, then treating the people with blue eyes harshly, relocating them to a corner,

Charlotte, where the situation with my niece went down, is the same place where Dorothy Counts historically entered an integrated school. Dorothy Counts was called n▮▮▮▮ to her face by fellow teenagers, not as a way of testing the word's power but with a full awareness of its meaning. One day, after the harassment of entering the school, she got sick. Understandably. Look at the photos and remember how much your teenaged self suffered over every social slight. I'm sure the white people in the background, taunting her, went on to become assistant managers, directors of communication, vice-principals, etc., much like Nazi supporters after the war went on to have mundane middle-class lives.

ignoring them. This exercise successfully makes a point about the arbitrariness of race and discrimination because of the disorientation it produces in people who are not used to being disadvantaged arbitrarily, people who are not accustomed to being unlucky.

Our present moment—of pandemic, of racial justice protests—is a collective disorientation that challenges our prior assumptions about normalcy, safety, and the status quo. White people are finally disoriented by the ubiquity of evidence and cases of violence against Black people. These cases proliferate. But white people are also disoriented by how rapidly things seem to be changing. A white person had a job, said something racist, and *poof*, the job was gone. That kind of disorientation is the crumbling of dominance, a kind of earthquake that leads to vertigo and collapse.

5. DISORIENTING EVIDENCE

Remember the last comment I mentioned from the poodle story: "This one person's lived experience is not statistically relevant. Anecdotal evidence may or may not be an outlier." The issue here is what constitutes valid evidence of racism.

Let's use an example from Claudia Rankine's *Citizen*.

You're at the drugstore and a white man darts in front of you with his items. The cashier informs him that you were next. He turns around, surprised.

I didn't see you, he says.

You politely suggest that he must be in a hurry.

No, he says. I just didn't see you.

Is this experience racist? It's pretty easy to dismiss, no? The man says he didn't see you. Done. Why go and make the incident out to be a microaggression?

To understand how difficult that question is for Black people to answer, try switching the terms. Imagine that you're explaining to a skeptical friend that you think Leslie is interested in you. She messages you a couple of times each week. You had coffee once. She's recently out of a relationship. She told you that. The evidence, even put together, seems thin. You can't cite gut feeling in a discussion of evidence, nor can you reference another time something like that kinda maybe sorta happened to you.

The difficulty of proving that an incident is racist, much

like proving the whiff of romance as substantial, is the pliability of evidence. *Of course* there are other explanations. The man who darts in front of you has reduced peripheral vision from advancing cataracts. Finding irrefutable evidence is like observing subatomic behaviour: the minute you observe the electron, it has shifted elsewhere. So I understand when some Black people say they're no longer going to talk about race with white people. They've had too many reasonable, Enlightenment-era conversations where they respect the wanton interpretations of others while being forced to defend their own. It seems to me that empathy is only possible if people are willing to suspend doubt, even temporarily.

Another issue with evidence is that the person in power determines whether it's valid or not. In 1798, Venture Smith's record of his life, his own life, had to be validated by certificate by five white men. Earlier in the eighteenth century, Phillis Wheatley required three prefaces, including an attestation signed by the governor of Massachusetts and seventeen white men, to prove that she indeed authored the work she claimed she did. Equiano's claim to be born in Africa is called into question because a white scholar trusts a birth certificate from Carolina over Equiano's word. We know from the birther conspiracy surrounding Obama's first campaign just how little Black people are trusted to be guardians of their own histories. The point here is that the evidence of Black people requires corroboration by white people to be believed by white people.

And yet another problem with evidence, or, more specifically, with substantiating a racist event, is that white intention is used to excuse white behaviour while little or no thought is given to the impact of that behaviour on Black people. White people will do their share of racial work when they habitually recognize the negative *impact* of their behaviour rather than excusing themselves for having neutral *intentions*. By shifting to impact over intention, they acknowledge, even prioritize, the feelings of Black people, the unfair disorientation that we are constantly contending with while they merrily continue their day.

There are other problems with evidence. When a white person, as in the poodle comment, isolates each of our experiences as unfortunate but anomalous, she is questioning our relevance as individuals. When she claims that we have misinterpreted a situation, she is questioning the sophistication of our mental faculties. Both of those acts are rooted in ideas on the inferiority of Black humanity: the first diminishes the value of an individual Black life, the second diminishes Black intellect.

As you can see by now, the need to "prove" racism is loaded with problems for Black people. There is no once-and-for-all piece of evidence that will stop the questions and doubt over racial discrimination. Even clear, recorded evidence does not convict police officers of crimes.

And evidence of what exactly? That racism exists? That one is socially literate enough to accurately perceive racism in a situation? I believe that many white people can accept the fact that racism exists, but for them it exists elsewhere, not in the daily drone of their communities and workplaces. So to identify it in a place where they can't perceive it or admit that it's possible is either a false claim or evidence of their ignorance. Neither of those explanations for their blindness is a feel-good. So fragility ensues, the enormous effort white people make to give alternate readings to evidence, to colonize reality, articulated or unarticulated, with *That was not racist. Maybe you're being oversensitive.*

I suggest that we stop asking, What's the proof? and instead ask, What's your experience? Proof elevates the modes of reasoning and the interpretations of white people. But, again, the experiences of Black people *are* the evidence, not the interpretations of white people.

Does this mean we believe that the incident in the drugstore is racist because a Black person says it is? Tricky, right? Well, chances are that the effect is racist, in that it triggers and coheres with other experiences in that Black person's life; so yes, it is being read as racist and those feelings matter. Replace the search for some kind of objective evidence (scientific, logical, statistical) and instead focus on the effect of an incident and most likely you'll find that the bewildering, disruptive, disorienting effect that the event has caused in the Black person's psyche needs to be addressed in addition to the structural and systemic issues that make such psychic violence possible.

I suppose what's beneath all these issues with evidence is trust. Who and what is assumed to be trustworthy? Who gets to skip to the conclusion? In a high school chemistry class, where I was within one point of an A+, I wanted to know what I was doing wrong. So, during a parent-teacher conference, my mother asked. The teacher explained that I was skipping steps and needed to show my work. I was pissed by that, because I was a kid who valued efficiency—skip grades, skip steps, get to the answer and the point. I didn't just move forward, I accelerated through life. So for the teacher to ask me to slow down ran contrary to my nature, and it also signalled that he didn't believe I had arrived at the answer through legitimate steps. He did not trust me.

To believe my word means that you trust me. And I won't lie to you if your trust matters to me. Each of us risks being cheated or hurt in this arrangement.

Both parents were furious when my niece told them she had been called a n███. But they differed as to how to respond. The white mother said they should speak to the school administration. The Black father, distrustful of admin, said my niece should handle the situation herself. They'd equip her, sure, but she needed to know how to deal with it.

On one hand, you have the belief in a system to make things better. On the other, the belief that the problem of race needs to be handled between individuals. Teach a kid how to fight if she's bullied—that line of thinking. She would, after all, be facing this throughout her life.

As I understand the story, my niece dealt with the issue herself. She told the girl, Don't ever talk to me like that. But no one was punished. I don't think the girl apologized. No solution would undo the disorientation. One girl tested a word on another. My niece tested a response. Together, at ten, they entered American politics.

TEN BULLETS ON WHITENESS

One can never really see into the heart, the mind, the soul of another.

—JAMES BALDWIN,
"The Black Boy Looks at the White Boy"

1. WHITENESS EXISTS

Whiteness exists as an institution. Institutions are generally abstract. They are visible in their effects but invisible in physical form, except by way of symbol. You'd have a hard time pointing to the state or to marriage, but you could point to their metonyms: a white man in a navy suit, the master bedroom. We sense whiteness because it organizes society and insists on conformity across time, but we don't always recognize the instruments it uses to uphold power. Moreover, the symbols of Klansmen, skinheads, and burning crosses are extremist caricatures of a more commonplace presence. As an institution, whiteness has systems (such as capitalism), operators (who occupy every leadership position), media (that exports images of Blackness), and products of the white mind.

Whiteness also exists as a cluster of ethnicities, not as a homogeneous, monolithic race. White people can accurately and confidently trace their ethnicities back to specific European countries by using state and family records in a way that many Black people across the Americas cannot without using DNA ancestry tests. Irish, Italian, and Jewish people were notably excluded from whiteness until fairly recently.

There is a difference between whiteness and white people. Yet I cannot resolve the difference as neatly as I would like. After all, white people uphold whiteness and transfer its crimes to institutions, processes, bureaucracy, to keep their hands clean in the same way that some wealthy people launder their assets. The institution of whiteness is better protected than white people themselves. The people are disposable in the ongoing machinery of this system. The power of institutionalized whiteness extends beyond the span of any individual life.

Do white people separate Blackness from Black people?

Perhaps white people should bear more responsibility for whiteness. I'm conflicted at the moment by how Black people carry the stereotypes of Blackness, even if we don't contribute to them, while white people can repudiate the history of whiteness as separate from themselves.

The bodies of some people are repositories of whiteness. Some bodies are hosts. Whiteness would have you believe that race and whiteness are separate and that race originates in the Black body. But no, race originates in the white imagination.

Exposing the existence of whiteness is important because invisibility renders it innocent. The existence of whiteness is obvious to Black people and white people alike, but Black people are daily aware of it while white people only occasionally need be—which is advantageous to white people and deleterious to Black people.

Depending on one's purposes, whiteness can be invisible the way God is invisible—enormous, conceptual, debatable, omnipresent. For anti-racists, it becomes something to dismantle or reject. Or it can be invisible the way a virus is—small and ubiquitous. At this level, it becomes something to manage, discuss, study. One feels no major threat until the viral load exceeds one's preparedness. The third way it can be invisible is not through any property of its own but through blindness.

When white people do not see their whiteness, they can claim that they—and the structures of the world—are "not racist" or postracial. They may be blind to themselves, but they are not blind to the racialization of others. Whiteness wishes that white people would remain blind to themselves and accept their experiences as typical of everyone's, so relations of dominance could continue unquestioned.

"The devil's finest trick is to persuade you that he does not exist," Baudelaire warned. Whiteness is most disorienting when it is undetectable.

2. WHITENESS CENTRES ITSELF

Whiteness imagines itself at the centre of everything it touches. Time itself begins in Greenwich and the Prime Meridian sets every point on Earth as east or west of London. Whiteness centres its face in a mirror that we all look into. Its political structures are the required template for how nations of nonwhite people organize themselves. Its subjectivity is both the supreme state and the default setting.

While I was in university, literary critic Harold Bloom published this audacious title: *Shakespeare: The Invention of the Human.* That's how one white man writes about another white man. Whiteness sets itself as the "god term," to be desired, pursued, and obeyed if you're white, or worshipped, emulated, and, yes—still—obeyed if you're not.

Default and *supreme.*

Those two words work hand in glove. We go from *default* (it would be redundant or fussy to identify white characters since their lives stand in for all lives, like *man* for *humankind*) to tenets of supremacist ideology (white characters are the *model* of all lives). Until recently, white characters were never identified as such in novels, perhaps because for a long time there were only white people in books. The desire for a monoracial world persists every time a writer does not need to state that a character is white.

Everything it touches.

Of all myths, I find Midas the most terrifying. I was a child when I heard it, and the thought of being touched and frozen into gold was as close to the concept of death as I could understand. Now, after living through a pandemic and 1990s sex education, I think it's the contagion that frightens me most. Whether the touch was uninvited or desired, it had the power to render me powerless. You can probably guess where I'm going with this. Whiteness, like

Midas's touch, turns everything into what *it* wants. It replicates its values and attitudes in you.

Here's another way to understand how the touch of whiteness works. On the Sistine Chapel's ceiling, the famous central panel, God's finger is an inch from Adam's. Most interpretations claim that this is God about to touch Adam, but I see it as the moment after God has touched Adam. The whole painting loads outward from that point. The touch of God connects man to the divine. The touch of whiteness was seen as a gift. Percentages of white blood mattered substantially to the working and social conditions of a Black slave. To have enough blood to pass as white meant mobility. The touch of whiteness, right in the middle of the painting, connects one to the electricity of power. Furthermore, as Adam in perfection is an extension of divinity, the touch of whiteness makes no distinction between whiteness and humanity. Its attributes become desirable (to have different hair is to have wrong hair). Its atrocities (say, stemming from the desire for superiority) are regarded as *human nature*.

3. Whiteness Values Itself

Whiteness has high self-esteem. It is confident.

On my first day in a Canadian school after moving from Trinidad, my teacher instructed a white boy to help me spell *journal* so I could print it on the cover of my exercise book. I thought, But wait, I know how to spell *journal*. I had almost won a spelling competition the year before (the word *nought* cost me). The white teacher made an assumption about my intelligence and the superior intelligence of the white boy. To make matters worse, whiteboy spelled *journal* without the *u*: *jornal*. And worse still, I'm ashamed to admit, I copied the incorrect version, although I knew better, because I trusted whiteness. I understood my island to be a speck in comparison with this great, advanced country, so I doubted my own knowledge. When my teacher spotted the error, she paused. She did not attribute it to the white boy, or to me, not directly. She did not correct it either. At home, I showed my mother and we inserted the *u*.

When white people say to me, You sound white, they mean it as a compliment. When Black people say it, they mean it as an insult.

Whiteness loves what it has. It loves having. It takes pride in its skyscrapers and beaches. My parents have been disappointed with every North American beach they have visited (just some dirty water, is their assessment). Many racialized immigrants react to whiteness's prized possessions and achievements with a perplexed, What's so special about that? North American cities can't compete with Asian cities in density, infrastructure, complexity, and energy.

Whiteness valuates itself like a stock about to hit market. It picks numbers out of the stratosphere. Western art is worth more than art from the rest of the world. Art by white people is priceless not because it displays rare talent but because it defines what talent is, even when the aesthetic values are contradictory—realistic, abstract, or non-representational. The art world pours money into the contemporary art of whiteness.

To be crude about the value of whiteness, consider the price of kidneys:

African kidney:	$1,000
Filipino kidney:	$1,300
Moldovan or Romanian kidney:	$2,700
Turkish or Peruvian kidney:	$10,000
US kidney:	$30,000

The price of a Black slave in 1850, adjusted for inflation, would be $12,000.

4. WHITENESS PRESERVES ITSELF

In historical narratives and current news, whiteness maintains a record of itself from its own perspective and destroys counter-perspectives, even if that means killing Black and Indigenous people to do so. This method of record keeping is legitimized through reductionist scientific slogans like survival of the fittest. Black and Indigenous people have not been the fittest, whatever that means, or had the best conditions, yet we have survived. I wonder whether our persistence is an affront to whiteness. Through various means and obstacles, from policing and incarceration to drugs to social segregation and moral humiliation, the active destruction of Black people is in service to the preservation of whiteness. After all, one can be preserved through one's fitness or through the destruction of one's rival.

Whiteness diffuses itself through the dominant episte-mological lens of the time, whether that be science or phi-losophy or art or religion. The records of whiteness are fixed with the most durable form of record keeping avail-able and disseminated by the most extensive media. Whiteness restricts who has access to these forms of preser-vation. By making it illegal for slaves to read and write, whiteness turned Black lives into vapour and kept those stories out of circulation.

5. WHITENESS ADAPTS

Preservation is how whiteness controls its story in the past and present; adaptation is how it prepares itself for the future. Whiteness adapts by changing rules, not by changing itself. It raises interest rates, lowers them. It raises prices. It lowers them. When I lived across from a gas station, I mon-itored price fluctuations to the decimal. Prices appear to be yo-yoing in response to market forces, but they are in fact within the control of people, real people who wash their pil-lowcases and make choices that preserve their wealth.

Here's another example. Whiteness can adapt to pres-sures in its surroundings by gentrifying neighbourhoods, which is its word for making the undesirable desirable, simply by entering a space. One of the most troubled postal codes in Canada, East Hastings in Vancouver, runs parallel to Gastown, one of the most desirable neighbourhoods. Old buildings were converted into lofts, cobblestone roads preserved, merchandise priced just north of affordability.

The urban professionals who live in Gastown move through that shared district with sunglasses and earbuds, insulated from the contrast.

Whiteness is like a melody where the tune stays the same but the words change. Think of how "Autumn Leaves" appears in contrafactum. (I like that word here because it sounds as if it means something else.) Alternatively, sometimes whiteness has to surrender its recognizable melody, but its chord structure remains the same. Slow it down, speed it up, change the genre, but in all these covers, the spirit of the song is the same. Dominance.

White people are creative, sure, but not more than other people on Earth. Creativity or intelligence is not the domain of a single race.

Whiteness, as an institution, is also creative in its strategies to remain dominant. Up to the middle of the last century, white people were still emboldened to state their racist ideas without evidence or repercussions. Now it has adapted to the climate of exasperated racialized people and a vocal generation with access to direct dissemination of its rage by claiming that it is not racist.

On *emboldened*: When I used to read my mother's poetry anthologies, I kept returning to Sylvia Plath, the most popular poet of the mid-century. I was always arrested by how casually she uses Black people for effect in "Ariel":

Nigger-eye
Berries cast dark
Hooks—

To every challenge and agitation of Blackness, whiteness finds a way to respond, even if the response is only a performance. It's a chicken-and-egg problem: Blackness responds with subversions and solutions to the agitations of whiteness, and whiteness in turn responds with craftier strategies. But whiteness is the chicken in all of this. The chicken dies before the egg.

Adaptability is among the most important attributes of our age because the rate of change is so steep. Travel agencies and video stores disappear. Phones go from rotary to Touch-Tone to flip to touch screen, which get outdated, supposedly, every couple of years. In management jargon: an institution that is adaptable and responsive will be nimble enough to survive. When that institution is coupled with the power to determine the rate of change, it becomes virtually unstoppable.

6. WHITENESS CONTRADICTS ITSELF

Adaptability causes whiteness to sometimes find itself in an uncomfortable position. Its escape methods can resemble contortionist manoeuvres. It promises a 0 percent interest rate on credit purchases, but in the dizzying fine print you discover that 0 percent means 22 percent.

Intersectionality is used by people of colour to expose how multiple identities complicate one's existence. But intersectionality functions in whiteness too. While the intersectional crossings of Blackness (+ gender, say) yield a decrease in opportunity, the intersectionality of whiteness

(+ religion, say) yields increased opportunities at best and niche opportunities at worst. Powers merge. Few things are more formidable than the intersection of white patriarchy.

Whiteness can be misogynistic while protecting white women.

It can speak a dialect of Christianity in public while behaving unscrupulously in private.

Whiteness is not uniform. It will accept new groups of people for its own preservation. As noted under bullet point 1, whiteness exists as a cluster of ethnicities, not as a homogeneous, monolithic race the way Blacks outside Africa are perceived to be. Occasionally, a group is designated next in line to be white. I never remember who. Black people are not in the line at all.

Whiteness is lawless. Even though it makes laws, interprets them, changes them, executes and exports them, it positions itself above its laws. Its laws serve its interests. Look into freeports.

7. Whiteness Is Powerful

We know how powerful something is from the ease with which it accomplishes its desires. Whiteness can do whatever it wants. To be fair, many white people can't, but whiteness can.

Because whiteness permeates the state, because the state, in fact, is constructed on white supremacist ideologies, whiteness has the power to start wars, destroy entire countries, peoples, to take what doesn't belong to it. Its kindergarten report card would say, "Whiteness is encouraged to regulate its emotions and behaviour. Whiteness is encouraged to share. Whiteness is encouraged to play nicely with the other children."

It's obvious that whiteness is powerful. The question is not so much whether whiteness is powerful but *how* powerful whiteness is.

Here's a hypothetical situation. Something goes missing from your house. The white child points to the Black child. The Black child points to the white child. Whom do you believe? I reckon that, without even speaking, the white child already has the benefit of credibility. Whiteness bestows innocence or good motives on its subjects; when one is freed of consequence, one has the power to act in any way one chooses.

Whiteness is so powerful that it can distort reality. It bends even the information we take in first-hand, information we observe with our senses, into whatever it wants. The testimony of a white person is so powerful that it is taken above recorded evidence. I'm thinking about the killings of Black people recorded on phones, which, given to any sighted person, would be a clear indication of the unprovoked, unwarranted murder of a defenceless and non-threatening person but is easily controverted by the testimony given by white men. Imagine a time before these recordings. Imagine a time when there is no device present. Whiteness bends the physical reality of the world. That's how powerful it is.

Whiteness can demonstrate its power through violence, but even in its weakest state its power outstrips others'. Some of the most egregious abuses of public trust occur when whiteness performs fragility. We observe this performance when a white woman calls the police to wrongfully accuse a Black person of law-breaking. The woman sobs into the phone, even though she was shouting at the Black person moments ago. She accesses the power of the state to support her, but really it's her whiteness coursing through a system. Her whiteness recognizes the dispatcher's and the officer's collaboration with whiteness.

One can see the dynamic of familiarity at the office, where a white person can mobilize whiteness to their advantage. The white candidate reminds the white hiring manager of herself, but she finds that the Black candidate, leaning too heavily on her credentials, doesn't quite fit, which is to say she doesn't seem personable. She asks, Can you see yourself having a beer with her?

8. WHITENESS OPPRESSES

Oppression and power are related. Oppression is a means to secure and maintain power. Whiteness partners with other agents to oppress others.

- Capitalism. Built on the labour of Black people, capitalism requires inequities to thrive.
- Colonialism. Whiteness replicates itself. It understands others by making others into itself. To call whiteness meddlesome would be an understatement. It leaves

countries worse than when it arrives. It extracts, dominates, confuses, then withdraws itself in an official capacity; that is, it withdraws from its responsibility, but it does not withdraw its influence. In present times, whiteness still likes to be everywhere, from inhabited Arctic regions like Alaska to tiny islands in the Pacific like Guam. America maintains over eight hundred military bases in foreign countries.

- Slavery. What is slavery but the domination of one group by another? One group remains human; the other is turned into a machine for labour. Slavery separates the mind from the body, enervates the former and exhausts the latter, until both are destroyed.

- Environmental plunder. In the name of enterprise, whiteness oppresses the natural environment, which is seemingly defenceless against human intrusion. Nature repays human plunder in its own time with natural consequences.

- Science. The application of science is not neutral. For much too long, medical research has taken the white, male body as the unit of humanity.

- Religion. Even the institution that professes the highest moral standard has been deployed by whiteness in the name of white supremacy and Black subjugation.

- Education. Beyond granting access to prosperity, the educational system is a site of acculturation into social structures. The power of the white professoriate—who knows all and to whom one must relinquish alternative epistemologies—is a way of locating trust and knowledge in the white mind. If university rankings are to be trusted, you would believe that no intelligence remains untouched by whiteness.

Instead of *oppression*, my father uses the word *domination*. *Domination* holds whiteness accountable for its actions, while *oppression* comes closer to describing what it feels like to live among whiteness and its agents. It's a slight difference, and simply a matter of point of view, but it's a small victory of the human spirit that I feel more oppressed than dominated.

The contradictory nature of whiteness means it can be oppressive and democratic simultaneously. It is democratic in its ideals and oppressive in its actions, without much need to reconcile the two; that is, it does not need to aspire to its ideals or confess the true nature of its actions.

9. Whiteness Takes Offence

Whiteness is *easily insulted*. The whiteness police would correct *easily insulted* to *sensitive*. But *sensitive* deflects us from the brutality of whiteness.

The response to insult is defence and denial. To be literal, on the state level, whiteness defends itself militarily. On the level of discourse, it deploys arguments to justify its necessity, its history of progress, while ignoring how that progress was achieved and at whose expense. White supremacist literature is an extreme example of white apologia.

On an interpersonal level, it defends itself from personal

complicity by deflecting racial activity to conservatives, to skinheads. Here's how that might sound. In response to the discomfort of these ten characteristics, a white person could say, *I'd never get away with saying such things about Blackness.* (True, but white people "got away" with such anatomies for centuries.) *I bet if he wrote about Blackness, it would be eulogistic.* (Probably largely so, as a corrective to common misperceptions.) *He's writing about racists, not me.* (Actually about a racist system that greases itself with us.)

And so we get into a spiral of perceived insult, defence from a position of victimization, and before you know it, the Black person is back in the troublemaker's chair.

Whiteness is easily insulted by calls to accountability. It is appalled by calls for justice because ethics has never constrained its behaviour before. Why should it now? Denial may be outright or it may be a distortion. Whiteness wants paintings of itself or selfies run through a filter—anything but the mirror. To see itself without distortion is unbearable.

10. WHITENESS IS OBSESSED WITH BLACKNESS

Dr. Flint, the slaveholder of Harriet Jacobs, author of *Incidents in the Life of a Slave Girl*, began sexually pursuing her when she was fifteen years old. Jacobs tried to free herself from his obsession—she fell in love, she ran away, she hid in her grandmother's attic for seven years while her children grew up. Dr. Flint retaliated against her attempts at freedom. He built an isolated cabin for her (and for him to "visit") in the woods. He sold her children. He cut her hair. He struck her. He tracked her down in New York and New England. Even his death did not stop his obsession. He vowed that Jacobs would never be free so long as he had descendants to own her. Whenever I teach Jacobs's autobiography, students are astonished by her master's obsession with her and her body. Why does he care so much?

Care.

The prevailing narrative is that whiteness is interested in the question of humankind. What is a human? Are all people human? But I'd contend that its obsession with Blackness does not lie in resolving the humanity of Black people but in the *certainty* of Black humanity and in exploiting it as a testing ground for the limits of human subjugation and endurance. What is the human capacity for debasement? With the persistent devaluation of Black life, whiteness asks, How much can another human lose? It asks, How much can I get away with?

The invisibility of whiteness—no, the blindness of whiteness—is so profound that whiteness relies on Blackness to understand itself. James Baldwin writes about the interaction between Blacks and whites as foundational to the American identity.

Defining the self in contrast to another entity is common. Teenagers differentiate their emerging preferences against their parents'. In Canada, the problem of national identity used to be acute, so we defined ourselves against Americans. We have health care. We are polite. Our universities are affordable. And if Canadians define ourselves against Americans, against white Americans who define themselves against Black Americans, then Canadians also require a stability of identity from Black people. Canadians are implicated in the condition of Black people in North America. We—Canadians, Americans, Blacks, whites, Indigenous peoples, as well as a host of ethnic peoples—share a continent. Our identities are historically entangled. The nervousness around this point causes white Canadians to situate themselves favourably in American history as, say, the Promised Land at the end of the Underground Railroad.

Definition by negation is problematic because it is relational. So, to wield some control over this process of identity formation, whiteness shapes all the things it does not want to be into Blackness. Whiteness is obsessed with its purity. More precisely, it protects its freedom to pick and choose which elements it absorbs. It plunders and absorbs features of Black creativity while refusing other parts. When I was in graduate school, Greg Tate published a book with a title that makes me smile to this day: *Everything but the Burden* (the subtitle is *What White People Are Taking from Black Culture*). Everything from fades to soul has been absorbed into the mainstream, and all of it is sold. And so Blackness enters the marketplace again. We buy ourselves as white people.

PART 2

Four to Eighteen Days

1. Moving

On the road again.

I'm moving again. I have thirty days to get out of my condo. So long, yoga pants of Vancouver. Hello again, toques of Toronto. That was corny. I've set up mail forwarding, cancelled my utilities, put my closet and bookcases on a diet. Am I forgetting anything? The moving company will get back to me with a firm pickup date. And then my furniture will mosey along the Trans-Canada Highway to country music.

I'm moving back to what people call *home*. Where's home? is such a tired question for immigrants. We are supposed to feel caught between the rock where we were born and the hard place where we live. The rock and the hard place drift apart, pulling our legs in opposite directions until we rip ourselves in two. You are supposed to show sympathy for our displacement and feel a touch of envy for our exotic rock. We are supposed to lap up your sympathy and acquiesce to your ownership of the hard place.

True, I've moved around enough to make the question of

home complicated. But I can make it simple for you. Home is where the money is. Where I work determines where I live. I've never had the luxury of choosing to live in a place while my bank account regenerates itself like a lizard's tail.

Anyway, I am moving back, if not home. I'm supposed to feel like a circle. While packing my blender into a box, I recognize myself in a squeezed half lemon drying out on the counter. I have more thoughts than feelings, the most dominant of which is, Where next? I throw the lemon in the garbage.

When I told my friend Jean Claude that I had decided to take the job in Toronto, he asked why, and I said, You know.

No, I don't, he said. Why?

The usual reasons.

Family?

No.

You're tired of this job.

I love this job.

Then why? he asked again.

And I said, Money.

Vancouver said they'd match the money.

Yeah, but Toronto would match the money plus more.

A smile began on his face. Oh, I get it.

I smiled back. It's pretty obvious, right?

Right, he said. You're a money whore.

Yo, I been poor. And my parents grew up poorer. Money is not negligible when at every juncture your opportunities are determined by family money. A plant's roots grow to the size of its pot. In my most lamentable moments, I bemoan how my potential was stunted by childhood constraints. I wanted to play violin, I wanted to swim, I wanted other encyclopedia sets, I wanted a microscope, I wanted to study abroad. I wanted so many things that most parents would gladly give their child if they could afford it. I wasn't asking for a Nintendo and ball shoes.

My parents, like so many immigrants in the script, did their best. No violin, but piano lessons from the church organist. For books, family trips to the library. For art and languages and everything else, there were Canadian public schools and domestic tuition. They signed all the forms I brought them.

I like ze croissant and ze baguette, huh-huh.

One of the perks of this new job in Toronto is that I get a research leave after one year of work. I've worked fifteen years without a sabbatical. To put that in perspective, professors get a sabbatical every seven years, meaning I'm twice overdue.

I'm thinking about moving to France. I know I haven't even moved to Toronto yet, so this restlessness is premature. Hear me out. I have no ties in France, meaning I could live anywhere, not just Paris or Marseilles. I could buy a supercheap place somewhere secluded, a hamlet overlooking a field. I'd be the only living thing in the house. There'd be arched mouse holes in the baseboard but no mice. I would make myself into the ogre of the hamlet.

The French hamlet idea actually started with research into a character. He's a developer whose interests took me to a number of real estate sites, and before I knew it, I couldn't distinguish the character's interests from my own. That character's name is Beckett.

Samuel Beckett moved to France. James Joyce did as well. Gertrude Stein. Henry James, Ezra Pound, F. Scott Fitzgerald, Ernest Hemingway, and George Orwell. All these anglophones left their familiar countries behind and moved to France. Beckett went so far as to write in French.

Black people have long found creative liberation in France. There's James Baldwin, Richard Wright, Josephine Baker, Nina Simone. At the end of *Between the World and Me*, Coates seems most free when he writes about the French and their salmon pants and the bright sweaters tied around their necks. All my visits to France have been without incident. My first time was pretty white, except for the day my friend and I emerged from the metro near Sacré-Coeur de Montmartre to a dazzling community of Blackness. Hairstylists, money transfer services, yellows and greens, head wraps. I saw more Black people there than I had seen during my whole trip.

Is the current francophilia just displaced anglophilia? Is any attraction toward a European colonizing power a cover for self-loathing? I'm not online researching houses in Morocco or Haiti or any former French colony with Black people, though I'd be less conspicuous in these places. I would never be an ogre among Black people. Yet I instinctively cast my future self as an ogre in France over a human in Guadeloupe. Is it possible that I can no longer live outside white contact, even at the price of a reduced life? It troubles me that an unexamined "good life" for me as a Black man means living alone or living white. Furthermore, the effect of living in the West so long is that isolation in the name of sanity is easier than integration.

My desire for France deflates upon this realization. I imagine the neighbours chasing me through the village with pitchforks, crying out, *Nègre, Nègre*. And when I correct them in my timid French, they are unable to see me as having more than an infant's intelligence, which, in their opinion, is more confirmation than rebuttal of what I am. I close my laptop for the night.

I'm ashamed to say it, but a few days later I'm back on the French real estate site.

I think I've figured out what's so appealing. As a Black man in France, sure, I'd still be visible, even more detectable because of my nervous French. But the flip side of that hypervisibility is that I'd be forced to reduce the surfaces of contact with the outside world. My language skills would prevent me from any engagement with complex subjects, would render me unable to hear, except by tone, the disapproval expressed about my being.

I make myself a cute little avatar on the real estate site. I choose my hair, my eyebrows, my complexion, my clothes. I set up alerts for isolated properties. I save properties to my favourites. There's a stone barn on the Spanish border, way up in the Pyrenees. No neighbours. I could renovate it into a house, no? I wind up the courage to write the real estate agent in French for more info. No answer. I write other agents. No answer. I write one agent three times, through different channels, and no reply. Out of a dozen queries, I get two replies. Maybe it's a sign that I shouldn't spend my savings on becoming an ogre.

I'm writing all these agents and not getting much feedback, which makes me wonder, Is there so much demand for these properties that potential buyers can be ignored? No, the houses stay on the market for a long time. Is my French incomprehensible? No, my partner proofread some messages. Is there a strike in France? Is it because I mentioned I was Canadian and they didn't want to deal with a foreign speculator? Is my name too English? Is there something wrong with me? You see how events that might seem innocent to white people always have another layer with us? Maybe my avatar with the dark skin might be causing realtors to ignore me.

So I go back to my profile and choose new skin, eyes, and hair. Presto, I am now a white man. This is my version of the dating site experiment where a Black woman used the same description but different names and profile photos

(Hadiya as a Black woman vs. Jessica as a white woman).
You can guess which profile attracted more responses. But
I can't go through with the race baiting. I just can't. Within
a day, my moral senses are tingling. Race switching feels

dishonest, no doubt, but mostly it feels like a betrayal of my
own life and my people, in the name of experiment. In the
end, I erase my face altogether.

After becoming invisible, surrendering myself to the
imagination of the realtors, whose default client would
probably be white, I get two responses. Quick and casual,
to be fair, but still, someone saw me.

The angry Black man restrains himself.

Back in reality, the moving company is also ignoring my
e-mails. The movers are scheduled to arrive at my place in
Vancouver in a few days, but I need some information to
coordinate my travel to Toronto. I call the company.

When will my furniture arrive in Toronto? I ask.

We can't tell you that, the service agent says.

Huh?

I mean, we can't give you an exact date. We can only give you a range.

Okay.

You're looking at four to eighteen days.

Lady, you crazy, I think. But I ask, Anything narrower?

Well, we'll know once the driver's on the road. We'll call you forty-eight hours before arrival.

I explain to her that I need to book a flight and make arrangements, so forty-eight hours doesn't give me enough time to beam myself from Vancouver to Toronto.

That's the best we can do, she says.

And what if I'm not there in time?

Then, I'm sorry, we'll have to charge you a re-delivery fee.

* * *

I book a flight for day 12 of the four-to-eighteen-day range. When the new owners take possession of my condo, I spend a week in Victoria so I can continue working in relative comfort. I arrange to have my new place in Toronto cleaned. I call the moving company for an update. Your furniture will leave Vancouver this week, but we can't tell you when exactly it will arrive. I board my flight. I stay at an Airbnb in Toronto for two nights. I call the company. Still four to eighteen days. I clean the empty condo again. I have Internet installed. I move into the empty condo. I buy a patio set from Craigslist. I position it in a corner of the living area. I eat my meals here. I Zoom-teach my classes here. I sleep on the floor in the bedroom with my puffy coat under my hip for padding. I call, but I have a hard time reaching the moving company. A week passes. Two weeks pass. It's been almost three weeks since I left Vancouver. I e-mail the moving company on Thursday. The truck will arrive on Sunday! I try to reserve the elevator. We need more notice, the building manager says. And we do not permit Sunday moves. We're sorry. Everyone is so sorry but not troubled.

What sustains me throughout this time is the recourse to leave a bad review of the company on multiple sites. The thought literally warms me at night.

Day 22. I finally reach the moving company. I explain that my building needs more notice to arrange a security guard and the elevator for moves.

The service agent says, I sent you a message with the Sunday delivery date.

That's not everything, I say. My building doesn't allow Sunday moves. And even so, you sent me a date but not a time range. I need a window to reserve the elevator. I can't reserve it for the whole day. And I need ninety-six hours' notice, according to building policy.

She says, You can't expect us to know how much notice you need. Each building is different.

I say, You'll have to re-deliver.

She says, There will be storage costs and re-delivery charges, because we have to subcontract this out.

I am holding the phone with one hand and clamping my

forehead with the other. Listen, I say. I've been trying to be flexible [cough, not an angry Black man] from the beginning of this process, but now your company is really straining my patience. On your end, please arrange re-delivery for Monday or Tuesday. On my end, I will book the elevator and arrange security. Those are our respective responsibilities in this transaction. I'm fulfilling mine. Please handle your business.

The customer service agent is quiet. I feel a surge of power after the machismo of my monologue. But it's not real power. It's just adrenaline, and adrenaline short-circuits me. If I don't sit down soon, I'll black out.

I ask, When can I expect to hear from you with a confirmation?

* * *

Anonymous
★ ☆ ☆ ☆ ☆

DO NOT use this company unless you're moving to an alternate dimension where time has no meaning. I've been waiting for my furniture so long that I've forgotten the colour of my couch. You'd have better luck putting all your belongings in a spoon and walking across the country. Plus they'll slap you with various hidden charges and staggeringly poor communication. The reps won't answer your e-mails or return your call for days. I wish I could draw a skull and crossbones across their logo. BEWARE!!!

I fantasize about incinerating the company with as much fire as anonymity allows.

It's not a rant, I tell myself. I have a moral responsibility to review this company. I must warn others. I liken myself to all the social media social justice warriors who bear witness, who record state violence, who are vocal about holding people accountable for injustice. Is this not an injustice?

I hesitate before clicking Submit. If my review is not about rage, then it's about authority. Leaving a negative review wrests power from the perpetrator and turns it over to the victim. The reviewer has the power to open a trap door and feed the one who is reviewed to the gators. Click Submit, says my left shoulder.

A tiny voice on my right shoulder, my Christian conscience, says, You've had your fun, Ian. You've vented. Don't click. I hear a replay of my voice during the phone conversation. My voice turns into a cold prairie when I'm angry. (I don't get angry.) (Not the way people recognize anger.) (I get irritated when dealing with nonsense, bureaucracy, policy.) The voice comes out when I'm doing business alongside my mother and she is not being taken seriously, when adjustments that are possible for others, like being reimbursed with store credit, are not extended to her. The voice comes out when I'm passed around like chattel among call centre representatives. The voice is controlled, logical, academic, surgical. It burns, but it's ice, not fire. I go from being a Black man to being a person with rights to being a machine.

My partner has a similar voice. I first heard it when we were in a sub shop and she was trying to fix her mother's roof from a different country and time zone. It's the voice of immigrant children advocating for a family member against a corporate representative. And more than that, it speaks on behalf of people who have been wronged by a network of systems that refuses to co-operate with our kind.

It is the voice that refuses to submit to anonymity, that stands up, swollen and bloody-mouthed, after being knocked down.

Canadian Idol

People rank moving as the most stressful life event, ahead of divorce and having children, and they rank public speaking as the greatest fear, ahead of death. I don't know if I believe that. I just know I have no furniture, I've been wearing the same clothes for days, there's a pandemic raging, it's literary festival season, and I have an event with Margaret Atwood in a few days.

I've met Atwood a few times. At a lunch event, when my collection of poetry, *Personals*, was shortlisted for the Griffin Prize, she put her hand on my shoulder, all atwinkle, and said, I enjoyed your reading last night. We met again when I was up for the Giller Prize. At the gala, I was at one table with my people and she was seated at the next table with her people. I asked her people for a photo with her, and they took the message via cupped hand into her ear and she beckoned me over. I won the prize later that night and dissolved into a total fanboy onstage when I saw her smiling up at me from her table.

Now, a festival in Calgary is celebrating its twenty-fifth anniversary by pairing authors for conversation. They asked me who would be my dream partner.

Margaret Atwood, I said.

Let's see what we can do, they said.

Atwood agreed.

The evening before the event, I watch a CBC documentary that begins with a montage of Atwood walking onto stages around the world to the adoration of crowds. "She's a cultural and literary rock star," says the voiceover.

The morning of the event, there's still no furniture in my place. It's been twenty-four days since I left Vancouver, fifteen since I last slept in a bed or sat in a comfortable chair. My setup for the event is a bookcase turned on its side. My laptop sits on a tool box to raise it to eye level. I take a shower, I put on a turtleneck, and wait in the virtual green room.

Atwood shows up on time, wearing red. Even her glasses are red. My brain involuntarily runs a search of all the times red appears in her work: the red shirt, a red fox, red smocks on the handmaids. I decide red must be her favourite colour. The room behind her is softly lit. I can't discern the purpose of the room. It's a sitting, living, reading, meeting, office room. She notices there is nothing behind me. She wants to know why. I explain that I'm moving. I tell her about the delays with the moving company.

Do you have a bed, Ian?

I have a sleeping bag.

Do you have a pot?

One. I have a knife too. And cutlery. I'm okay.

As I explain the moving situation, she gets progressively more disturbed by the course of events. Her line of questioning is insistent, her attention dizzying—downright disorienting. She is not loud or forceful in the least, but when her attention is on me, I am unable to steer the conversation away from her curiosity. Hers is the kind of magnetism where you are not so much captivated as held captive until she decides to release you.

They said they'd deliver in four to eighteen days, I say. Now we're on day 24.

Her mouth drops a little. What's the name of this company? she demands.

I hesitate.

Do you want me to make a phone call to these people?

No, no, I say. But I bet you're very good at being taken seriously. I'm sure you'd be able to get things done.

Have you dragged them on Twitter?

Not my style.

Where do you live?

I tell her.

I know someone in the area. They can deliver some food to you.

I can't take charity.

It's not charity. It's just food.

Still, I can't. But thank you.

My armpits are wet. I'm glad I'm wearing a dark colour. It's not that I don't have money. I could set myself up in relative comfort, but habits of frugality are hard to shake.

Why buy another plate when I have plates in the back of a truck?

She asks again, slowly: Do you want me to make a phone call, Ian?

The way she asks, like the Godfather, shoots panic through me.

I say, Please don't. Please. You're putting me in the position of defending my oppressors.

She tenses her lips. Maybe it's a smile.

I'm afraid of what you'd do to them, I say. And I want my stuff delivered undamaged.

The public conversation goes well. Atwood is her usual witty, assured self. I drop my voice when I call her Margaret. I really want to say, Ms. Atwood, but she has set a tone for the evening that would make such formality comical. She has practically offered everyone a drink. Stay, relax, get comfortable, she is saying. Let me tell you a story.

She tells stories about editing poets I read in the library stacks. She has been around long enough to relate to everything I say. I read a poem about forgetting. She reads one about remembering. I talk about wearing one pair of Velcro shoes throughout my PhD. She talks about bell-bottoms and beehives and miniskirts. The moderator asks us what we were doing when we were twenty-five. I was about to start a job in Massachusetts and discover what being a Black man in America was all about. She nods. She tells a story about going for a walk in Cambridge and ending up at a Vietnam protest.

This event takes place the week after her eighty-first birthday.

How old are you? she asks me on air.

Forty-one, I say. Half your age.

Oh, you're young. You think you're old, but you're not.

I wonder if she means *wise*. The unsent moving company review flashes through my head.

By the time she was my age, she had written, without exaggeration, about twenty books. I have written five. This one here is book six.

She tells us that when she was around my age, she moved seventeen times in one decade.

My mind skips back to her concern in the green room. She wants to free my furniture. In my head, a baritone sings, *Go Down, Moses. Let my furniture go.* (Onscreen, in a display of impressive flexibility, she pulls her feet into view and, lo, she's wearing red Santa Claus slippers. Red. Confirmed.) The person she is onscreen confirms what I admire about the person she is in my imagination: a natural ire rises up in her at injustice, small or great. We could call this *being principled* or *holding the world accountable to principles*. If you say that you are going to deliver furniture by a certain time, deliver it by that time. It's that quality of being principled, writ large, that translates into her feminism and commitment to environmental conservation. Writ small, it translates into alleviating inconveniences. The difference between Atwood and me lies somewhere in this point. I am prepared to suffer. I expect a certain measure of it. She is prepared to change things.

Case in point, there's a time lag afflicting the event moderator. In the silences, I lean my ear toward the monitor, urging him to speak. Atwood fills the silences to give the moderator language.

After the event, we're in the green room again. She asks if I will be okay.

Yes.

Are you sure? Do you want a care package? Or an onion? Just say the word.

I have onions.

When she says good night, the darkness behind her seems enormous.

I cannot ask the questions that spring to mind as she is slipping away. They are too delicate. How does she sleep since her partner, Graeme Gibson, died? I mean the question quite literally. On which side of the bed? Does she still keep his pillow there? At what point does his smell leave the mattress, the room, the house?

I also cannot ask these questions because she is gone.

In screenshots of the event, she is pale against a black

background. I am dark against a white wall. She looks like a still from a film. I look like I'm trapped in a passport photo.

* * *

Afterward, charged with adrenaline, I march around the unfurnished condo, humming "Hungarian Rhapsody." My parents bought me a cassette of Liszt as a child and I played it in the background as I read my mother's anthologies. My condo is too small for my marching, so I take to the streets and walk through cold rain. When I've tired myself out, I return home, towel-dry my puffy coat, and tuck it under my hip as makeshift mattress padding. In my dream, someone keeps singing "where nothing is real," a line from "Strawberry Fields Forever." I think it's Atwood, but I can't find her. I encounter two mirrors in a bathroom. In one of them, I look great. I'm in focus, my hair's shiny, each curl is defined, there's a bubble of light in each eye, and, interestingly, I appear lighter, or not exactly, just more orange. In the second mirror, I looked like a Black guy shot on film with poor lighting and no flash. In the dream, I am surprised to discover that people recognize me as the man in the first mirror when I recognize myself as the man in the second.

MARGARET ATWOOD   IAN WILLIAMS

People want Atwood to blurb their books, to retweet them, to say they're geniuses, to bless them and their children. They want years of one-way familiarity and intimacy reciprocated. But that would make me anxious. I don't want long late night conversations about the state of literature or spontaneous phone calls where I ask her whether I should buy the green pants or the brown pants. I don't substitute her for my own mother, who, when I told her about the Atwood event, was stoic. Make sure you do something with your hair, she said.

What do I want from Atwood? The impossible. I want her alive forever. But I cannot preserve her in my head, let alone in the world. In the green room, I asked how she was managing during the lockdown. She told me she's got a backyard with various heating contraptions. She said I should get a pair of thermal-reflective gloves. She said when things get better, in six months she predicted, I should come over.

Oh dear, I said. I'll have to bring a pound cake.

Something like that, she said.

2. MOVED

The puppet appears

On my forty-first birthday, before all this nonsense with the move, I received a large box from my friend Myronn, an American poet. Inside the box was a card, *Read this first*, sitting on mounds of bubble wrap. The card actually gave away what was in the box: *I remember our conversation about the one you saw in Prague but didn't acquire.*

What I wanted so badly in Prague was a puppet of Icarus, hanging mid-flight from the ceiling of a puppeteer's shop. I considered buying the puppet for a long time. It was the size of an infant, dressed in a red shirt and blue shorts. I thought about it while sightseeing. I went back to the shop the next day. In the end, I was financially prudent and persuaded myself that the puppet was out of my price range and that shipping would be too costly. In place of the puppet, I took a photo. I used it as my Skype avatar for years. Skype was how Myronn and I communicated because he was always away. Or I was.

Sure enough, inside the box was a puppet of a Black man with bushy moustache and eyebrows. He's wearing a leather shirt that is frayed at the bottom over a mustard skirt. He's holding something in his hands, an axe maybe.

It took me a few days to realize that I'd misconstrued that. On closer inspection, he's holding a flute.

He's an artist.

I named the puppet Anonymous.

The puppet immigrates

The puppet, Anonymous, was born in a village in Tunisia. It journeyed from Tunisia to Morocco to New York to Maine to Vancouver and eventually—WHEN WILL MY FURNITURE ARRIVE?—to Toronto, where it will finally rest on top of a bookcase, next to a plant and a prize. The puppet's travels shadow Myronn's and my own.

The journey that this puppet took is familiar to academics. Myronn taught in Morocco for about ten years. Jobs in one's area of specialization are scarce. Competition is fierce. One goes where there's work. The puppet has endured various puppet-sized difficulties at each dislocation. It was hard to find a box big enough for it and the right kind of protective padding. Familiar problems. What really makes it special to a Black academic, though, is the journey across the ocean.

Anonymous Ancestors

I took a photo of Anonymous sitting on my shoulder and sent it to my partner. She said it looked like me. I sent it to a friend in Korea. He said the same thing.

I looked closely at the puppet's face. We're often the last to see resemblances between ourselves and others. I denied looking like my mother until time drew two marionette lines down my cheek. And same with my father, until I bought a pair of velvet pants and recalled—with horror—his velvet pants in a photo album from the seventies. The puppet has an elongated face and neck, large eyes, and a moustache. I've been rocking one too for the last few months.

Okay, so I recognize my face, yes, the skin, the Africanness touched by Europeanness. Then I note something more—the only word I have for it is *familiarity*. Anonymous could have been a simple doll, but instead it was made into a puppet. There's a place for strings to attach to its head, but—I looked—the places where the other strings go are hidden.

People have interpreted the slender, narrow sadness of my face as Ethiopian. It's the kind of guess they make when they intend to compliment me by whitewashing my Blackness. To trace my face backward, I flirted briefly with Ancestry.com, but it just chops me up into percentages. When people do these tests on the commercials, they get excited by the famous relative or the surprise ancestor of another race. The second narrative makes people cover their mouth: you're not the person you thought you were.

I'd like to know more. I'd like to know what my percentages were thinking and eating and wearing in 1720. I'd settle for a drawing of their faces. Hell, I'd settle for a name.

I make the mistake of trying to investigate my background once more. And again, I shut my laptop with the crossword feeling of having gotten some clues but no completion.

It would help to know who I'm looking for. I suppose I'm looking on my mother's side for the man who left her his skin, to see if I can find the woman he loved, raped, desired, what's the word, reproduced with, so that I could, I could what, so I could have a name and a face. Finding the woman is impossible. She has been erased. Finding the man is hard because there are many men like him. He is overrepresented in the records.

Imagine yourself in a version of this erased Black woman's life. Imagine yourself as an ancestor to your descendants. Everything you currently struggle with and fret over has vanished, and when your descendants look back, if they're lucky, they maybe find your name. It's a glimmer, no? But don't you wish that a great-great-great^n grandchild could see your face and say, I look more like her than my mom. What funny clothes she's wearing! She was a financial adviser? She wore a lot of red? She got divorced? She lost a child to an overdose? She died thousands of miles from the farm where she was born? And after assembling these pixels into an image of a human, wouldn't you want that descendant to know what man did you wrong and got away with it?

Here's the truth about looking for a white ancestor. I want to find him so I can track down his descendants and see how wealthy they are, how mobile, how many passports they hold, how ignorant they are of me, how slavery has been used for them like a disposable straw, useful at the time, utterly forgettable now that they're nourished.

A friend who shall remain anonymous messaged me about his unstable ancestry. Ancestry databases update their results periodically—surprise! you're not the person you thought you were!—and the effect of your reconstituted racial composition can be disorienting after you've made peace with your prior identity.

Anonymous: BTW, these DNA tests keep changing slightly. Now I'm more Cameroon than Nigerian.

Me: Yeah? I don't know what to make of these tests. I started at 20% Nigerian and now I'm 50% but I'm also getting whiter. You been to Nigeria?

Anonymous: No. I want to go now because of the DNA result. I was 30% Nigerian. Now I'm 20%. Are you from Mali as well?

Me: I think I have some Mali. I have to look again.

Anonymous: I'm 10% from Mali.

Me: Great?

Anonymous: I'm really happy about this. Remember the guy a few blocks over I thought was a musician? I run past his house in the mornings.

Me: What about him?

Anonymous: I think he's moving. His apartment seemed

emptier, but the keyboard is still front and centre and
the big framed watercolour is still on the wall.

Me: Are you gonna knock on this white guy's door one day
or what?

Anonymous: Haha. It's so not that deep. But I still really
want to see his place and I do wonder if he's actually a
musician. He wasn't sitting at the keyboard today. No
one was there. But the lights were on.

Me: I'd love it if he were a DJ.

Anonymous: And it would be great if we randomly became
friends.

Me: You sound like you're in kindergarten.

Anonymous: BTW, where in Europe?

Me: All over. Scotland, Ireland, France, Italy, or Spain.
Don't remember now.

Anonymous: I'm 15% Scottish. I'm not Italian.

Me: The rape happened. Not just historical allegations.

Anonymous: Well . . . clearly. I'm 20% Norwegian. The hell?

Me: I expected Portuguese stuff.

Anonymous: That too.

Me: Do you feel any connection?

Anonymous: Nuts. Europe is all rape.

I feel nothing.

Me: The white folks got around though they like to make
us seem like animals.

Nigeria and Norway. Your next trip.

Anonymous: When they raped us . . .

I'd like to see Nigeria.

There was French in my first DNA result but none now.
It was replaced with Russian.

Me: Russian?!

It's weird how quickly we adjust our history based on the new results. Like our attitude toward the new country softens.

Anonymous: Mine doesn't. To me that tragic . . . history of slavery and subjugation is even more real now.

It's literally in the blood, in the genes.

Me: What is whiteness doing inside of us—that feeling.

Nobody invited it in.

Anonymous: All those different ethnicities of Africans. All over the continent.

All those women being raped. It's really disgusting.

Me: And no way to connect with the original Blackness.

Nigerians won't claim us.

Anonymous: There are worse things than death.

Me: Orphaned by Africa. Raped by Europe.

Anonymous: I've been to Ghana, but I can't go . . . and say, love me.

Me: Ethnic tourism.

Anonymous: Or Mali, Cameroon, Senegal, Benin . . .

Me: Right. All we have is this continent. And they're shooting us up.

What a predicament!

OK. I'm gonna go for a run myself. Burn off some of this feeling.

Anonymous: It's really awful.

And the musician doesn't know I exist.

Me: One day you will knock on this white man's door

Anonymous: and say you don't know me

Me: but I know you.

Moved

The puppet Anonymous was the only enduring gift I received in the Year of the Pandemic. I remain moved by the sentiment and the expense.

When I was preparing to move back to Toronto, I packed it in a box of its own with yellow pillows on either side. It spent weeks in a loading facility, then in a truck with the other cargo, and then in a warehouse, before finally reuniting with me. It survived the journey unbroken and now it crowns my bookcase. Okay, the last part was premature. Anonymous is still in a warehouse somewhere. There is a chance that it might arrive broken or, worse, be lost forever.

3. THE MOTIONS

Sorry I am late

I call the moving company. I learn the location of the warehouse where my furniture sits, awaiting delivery. Brampton. It's where I grew up. I consider a heist.

Toronto enters another lockdown. The days shorten. It snows.

For some reason, I take to watching DJs play electronic dance music on YouTube. The videos are from our former world. There's no way anyone would tolerate the moist skin of strangers making contact with their own these days.

Now, while making dinner in my one pot, I watch DJs

play to crowds. I adjust the knobs of my cooktop like the dials of a mixing board. I dance when the beat drops. I eat, watching the bodies more than my food, and sometimes I pass out in my sleeping bag (an upgrade) while they continue to shuffle with the infinite energy of youth. These videos can be hours long.

Solomun is the DJ that started this phase for me. He too seems to come from a former world. He's a heavyset man, born under Eastern bloc Communism, the kind of presence one associates with bearded loggers and the proletariat. When I saw the clip of him remixing "Sorry I Am Late" by Kollektiv Turmstrasse, I sent it to every friend who texted me that day. In the video, Solomun charts a funky brass line by fluttering and chopping his hand through the air. He sips from a glass of wine. He's not the kind of man you expect to dance, but he does, with small, delicate gestures. He pinches his thumb to his finger. He waves his expressive pinky. The crowd adores him. The best parts of his videos are the moments when he dissolves from DJ into audience. Even among the crowd, he's so enraptured by the music that the audience appears incidental. He'd make music even if he was alone. I imagine him as a boy, spending many evenings in his parents' living room, conducting imaginary symphonies. Am I drawn to house music lately because I've been stuck at home, in this holding pattern, for so long? It captures both the monotony and the thrill of days in the house. One song blurs into another. It's hard to know where my workday ends and my personal life begins. I toggle between Outlook in one tab and WhatsApp in another.

House music isn't an outgrowth of shimmering European salon music. It emerged in the 1980s from Chicago's Black underground club scene. The term *house* is probably an abbreviation of Warehouse, the genre's birthplace and home to queer clubbers. From Chicago, house spread across North America to Europe. In a way, the spread of house music is no different from the mainstreaming of Black production: take the gold, take the style, take the slang; discard the people.

Surreal

Before this current phase, I assumed that DJs played in back-alley clubs where lasers strobed over sweaty bodies. But on YouTube, they spin in sublime locations. Imma claim that I've been there. I mean, is this virtual travel much different from the shallow ways we've been travelling this millennium—from snapping a selfie in front of the *Mona Lisa*? I have danced with these DJs atop a tower in Amsterdam while the sun sets, aboard a pirate ship in Ibiza, before the horseshoe stairway of Château de Fontainebleau, on the peak of Sugarloaf Mountain in Rio, so high up the clouds wrapped us, on the terrace of the Revelin Fortress among the red roofs of Dubrovnik. Alls I need is my HDTV to turn the red roofs of Croatia into the magic carpets of an acid trip.

The DJs who take me to these scenic places are them-selves sights to be seen. There's Solomun, the imposing conductor with the delicate gestures. Hot Since 82, the DJ I saw in Ibiza and Croatia, is a stunningly handsome man with a sleeve of tattoos, who wears his shirt unbuttoned into a deep V. Idris Elba, who played me a solo show in Amsterdam, needs no description. Boris Brejcha is a skinny man who wears a horned carnival mask. The mask has an impish smile and a steep nose. The first time I saw Boris (we tight now), I thought he was snorting coke through a secret tube in the mask. He was such a different person when he wore it. And he was wearing a shirt that said *Cocaine Cowboys*. The truth shamed me, though. When he was a boy, he was badly burned during a military air show disaster in Germany. His face is scarred. You never know where people are coming from.

Perhaps, at some point, the functional masks of the pandemic will morph into carnival masks and we'll all walk around not just masked but gloved, costumed, not an inch of skin showing. Would people interact differently if they didn't know the race of the person under the mask?

I have a dream

My mother says that I should come and stay with her in Brampton. Why are you suffering? You have a bed over here.

I tell her that my furniture will arrive any day now. I have faith.

What's in the background? she asks.
Music.
Turn it down.

Honey Dijon is a Black woman who deejays with fierce concentration and Shiva-limbed busyness. Every once in a while she backs away from the equipment and throws her hand up as if she has done everything possible to contain the music before letting it burst upon us.

More than other DJs, she seems to be interested in something apart from our pleasure. She doesn't empty words of semantic meaning. Instead of *dance, dance, dance,* she'll mix in *focus, focus, focus.* Her set in Melbourne, from 2018, begins with Stevie Wonder singing "I wish" a cappella. There's nothing to wish for, I think, compared to the disease, unrest, and wildfires of this summer. I had furniture in 2018. After a few moments the beat comes in, the tempo speeds up, a cross rhythm drops in, and the music unfolds in the fluid yet numbing way of house music. Metaphor of our days. Halfway through the set, though, the music recedes and Martin Luther's voice rises. He has a dream. His voice reverberates like it's haunting itself. The crowd erupts at the climax, then music floods in and he's forgotten. At the end of Honey Dijon's set, words seize our attention again. The last sounds are a woman's voice: "Just stopping by to let you know I won't be needing your lil' dick services any longer."

Honey Dijon is a Black trans woman. Aesthetics and politics are not separate.

* * *

I order a second pot, eight quarts large, while listening to Solomun's Boiler Room set in the next Chrome tab. The second-to-last song in the two-hour set is called "Horny." Between that song and the final one, he puts on his head-phones for a few moments then takes them off. The final song is "Hoping."

I used to wonder why DJs are so fussy with their head-phones. Sometimes they hang them around their neck. Sometimes they press one side against an ear. Sometimes they wear the full set. I discovered that they are able to listen to two songs at once in order to beat-match the present track with the upcoming one. Unlike the rest of us, caught up in the moment, DJs occupy both the present and the future.

Any day now I will have my sit-stand desk, my silver bench. I will have a gigantic pot of soup on the largest burner. I survey the empty room and conduct the furniture into various arrangements. Two bookcases here, three there, a couch in the corner for naps, a desk facing the window.

I had a dream

In the past, when I lived in Calgary, I went through a dance phase. I'd walk to work with headphones on, enter my office, and dance like Ellen (cancelled) to start the day. Then I'd sit down and write *Reproduction* for hours. I suppose dance phases counteract periods of increased still-ness—lockdown, sitting, confinement to screens.

In the early days of the first lockdown, back in Vancouver, my partner and I slow danced to Billie Eilish whisper-singing "I had a dream I had everything I wanted."

Before that, between the South Korean wave and the North American wave of the pandemic, I danced with my buddy and goddaughter to Dua Lipa's "Don't Start Now." In twenty years, we had never. In both cases, our bodies were anticipating restraints.

Personally, I am of the school that everybody can dance but not everything will be recognized as dancing. To dance, just find a song you like, pick a body part, and keep the beat. And because we associate dancing with personal expression, which itself involves a kind of freedom, you'll soon want to do more than keep the beat.

How do you teach someone to be free?

When postracial believers proclaim that freedom is there for everyone, you just have to take it, I remain as unconvinced as a wall-hugging dancer. If you have been socially controlled and disciplined in your desires to the point of total disconnection from your body, you're bound to be skeptical when someone tells you, C'mon, just dance. Likewise, for someone unaccustomed to freedom, shaped by the stereotypes, brutality, threats, confrontations, and shame of race, seizing freedom means rejecting the very skeleton of your identity

Can you hear that?

Bro, that's corny. You know we can't hear jack.

Listen.

Stop being corny.

Still no?

A white man is encouraging you to dance to music that only he can hear through his headphones. So surrounded is he by "We Are the Champions" in his noise-cancelling headphones that he cannot hear anything beyond the bubble, not your explanations, not your protests, not the traffic approaching you on all sides. To him, you appear to be dancing to the wrong song. To you, he appears to be dancing to your endangered life.

My car arrives before my furniture. I had loaded it onto the truck clean in Vancouver and now it returns to me covered in mud and a mohawk of snow. I file a claim with the company. Within twenty-four hours, someone writes back apologetically. Get the car washed, send us the receipt, and we'll reimburse you.

Speaking of reparations, I am still in an empty condo. I await the things that belong to me.

Between Us

My partner is Asian. I am Black. Or she is Taiwanese and I am Trinidadian. Or she is American and I am Canadian. She speaks English, Mandarin, and French—sometimes all in one day. I speak English comfortably and French longingly.

My brother is Black, as you know. His wife is white, as you know. He is Trinidadian turned Canadian turned American. His wife remains American.

How is it that neither of us ended up with Black women?

This question occupies me periodically. Even if you believe that I shouldn't trouble myself with it—love is love, the heart wants what it wants, and so on—you still have to admit that we are conditioned to see pairs that resemble each other. In America, 90 percent of people who marry do so within their race. Only 26 percent of Black women are married, compared with 48 percent of all women in the United States. If those two numbers say anything, it's that you expect to see me with a Black woman and that many Black women are available, therefore— And here the question reasserts itself.

Depending on who you ask, people in interracial relationships can be interpreted as self-hating, race-betraying, whitewashed, and/or privilege seeking. In Vancouver, my partner and I got the full gamut of looks, from encouragement to surprise to disapproval, from people inside and outside our races. I reckon it's the same with my brother, depending on the American neighbourhood.

Because race is typically cast as an ongoing struggle between Black and white people, what I think surprises people in my brother's case, down in the South, is that there can be intimacy between the two races. In my case, the surprise lies in the combination of me and my partner; people pause when they see evidence of interracial intimacy unmediated by whiteness. *Interracial*, to most people, refers to Black and white, usually a Black man and a white woman. Chiayi and I are a provocation, a curiosity. And, to be fair, sometimes we're unremarkable.

Did something go wrong in my childhood? Do my brother and I have higher degrees of openness? Doubtful. There was a period when I said I would only date immigrants, people who knew a culture outside North America. Those were lean dating years. When I trace my life, I understand the forces that led to my racialization. Some of these involve white people. Many do not.

The movements of my life, from Trinidad to Canada to Asia to America and back to Canada, do not conclusively answer the question of how I came to be with my partner, but they do make another important point. Even when whiteness is decentred, there remain innumerable tangled racial dynamics between and among racial groups. In Trinidad, Blacks and Indians vie for political control of the country. In homogeneous parts of Asia and Europe, the Black foreigner remains an object. In America, Black people from elsewhere negotiate their relations to African-Americans. And so on and so forth. Frankly, there are too many combinations to map here.

TRINIDAD: HOMEBODY

In Trinidad, my age and innocence did not preclude me from being racialized. I understood, for example, a categorical difference between Blacks and Indians. While I was being seen and not heard, I overheard adults having dull political conversations about which way the Indians would vote or about policies that would favour one group over another. What I didn't understand, I sensed: Blacks and Indians practised a form of racism on each other to ward off a more fundamental and sinister racism that had to do with white people. In their joint fear of and reverence for whiteness, I beheld a unifying force, the way feuding children put down their sticks when a more formidable bully enters the playground.

I understood that Portuguese and Spanish people had soft hair and lived elsewhere on the island, places I have never needed to spell until now—Morvant, Lopinot, Arima, Mayaro. Chinese people looked different from us but spoke with Trinidadian accents.

I understood that mixed-race people, most often Indian and Black, had their own category—*Dougla*. I understood colourism. Light-skinned women got jobs as bank tellers.

The flight attendants who welcomed us aboard flights between Trinidad and Tobago were fair and young. That combination was so frequently admired that I came to learn that these women were *pretty*. It was like learning the blond + skinny combo in North America. I used to correct lazy assessments of *cute* and *hot* with, No, you mean she's blond and skinny. That's not the same as pretty. I've stopped. I'm worn down these days.

I understood from TV that white Americans lived in a different world from us Trinidadians and that Black Americans lived more like the white Americans than like us. I heard that white people and Black people in America didn't get along, but on TV the Cosby family was as happy as the Keaton family, so it didn't worry me. I had marbles and G.I. Joes to collect.

I understood that British whiteness differed from American whiteness. The aura of the English colonial presence still lingered, decades after Independence. Our formal pronunciation leaned toward British English rather than twangy American English. Same with our spelling. My mother announced teatime and suppertime (still does). Football over soccer. Cricket over baseball. Lady Di over Madonna. Oxford over Harvard. I was one of those colonial kids who lined the street in 1985 to see the Queen roll by in a black car. My mother wanted to do the same twenty years earlier in 1966 (but didn't/couldn't).

Trinidadians understood the cool ferocity of white British imperialism, its unshakable dominion over us. We felt allegiance to English ways but also palpable relief that white people were for the most part gone, except around

Carnival time. It was like the freedom from the disapproval of a stern grandparent who didn't live with us. We felt the aura of whiteness, rather than its presence. There existed households like mine that were split down the middle between the two cultural powers, so when my father decided to emigrate from Trinidad, my mother was pro-Britain, where two of her sisters were nurses, while my father was pro-America because it promised him opportunity.

In the end, they compromised on Canada.

Over their lifetimes, my father would become disenchanted with the United States while my mother would continue to watch royal weddings and buy commemorative magazines of royal baby pictures.

I felt secure in Trinidad. There was physical danger, sure. People drowned or got hit by cars. There were monsters that sucked your blood if you were out at night. That was part of the reality of childhood. I suppose I felt safe from racial violence. I picked up from overhearing adults, from the kids who spent summers abroad, that there was something large and powerful that didn't like me. But at least it was elsewhere.

Then we moved elsewhere.

CANADA: BODYCHECK

At the first place we lived, I had the bizarre perception that all Canadian adults were white but kids could come in multiple shades. This was in Brampton, a suburb-turned-city northwest of Toronto. Back then, in the late 1980s, teachers, librarians, salespeople in department stores, bank tellers, bus drivers, catalogue models, every employed adult with the exception of church people—white. In Trinidad, everyone from our politicians to police officers, bankers to bakers, shared a physical familiarity with me; I was never disoriented or displaced by one racial group dominating another.

I crept toward a pernicious logical conclusion. Everybody non-white in Canada had to be from elsewhere, therefore everybody non-white had less claim to the country. Everyone non-white should defer. There wasn't a thought to people preceding white settlers, Canada's Indigenous people, apart from a spiritless unit on the Inuit in elementary school. They were swept aside with the same temporal irrelevance as dinosaurs. Extinct. What would become of the rest of us? Would our parents grow extinct? Would they go "back home" as they threatened—or perhaps dreamt? Maybe my non-white friends themselves would grow into white people.

Apart from the white blanket, there was an ideological covering over Canada. Canadians wore modesty—genuine in its insecurity but false in its self-chastisement—as a protective identity, especially when it came to Americans. We played the part of America's younger, polite, simple-minded, hockey-playing sibling. Too innocent for racial awareness, let alone discrimination. Canadian innocence persists, to a degree, to the present. This positioning of moral superiority over Americans shuts down dialogue about Canada's own discriminatory practices against numerous ethnicities. So humble-proud are we of our beloved status internationally that we uphold the Multiculturalism Act, the inclusion of POC, as a domain where we finally beat the Americans at something. But everything that is possible in the US is possible in Canada. Shootings. Poor Black areas. Suspicious looks at Black bodies. Kids streamed into technical futures instead of academic ones. It's all here.

My family moved when I was in middle school to a more affordable area of the city, meaning more diverse. Those streets had kids from everywhere. Indian kids, Pakistani kids, Vietnamese, Chinese, Black kids from across the Caribbean (not too many Africans and fewer African-Americans), immigrant white kids from Italy, Portugal, Poland, waspy white kids, mixed kids, phenotypically unidentifiable kids. The baseball or street hockey teams resembled a future-friendly multicultural world. We were a drawing of diversity.

Over the years, Brampton has since undergone a radical transformation. Like animals sensing a tsunami, white people fled Brampton as Indian and Pakistani immigrants moved in. By the most recent census numbers, the three largest groups are South Asians at 44.3 percent of the population, Europeans at 26 percent, and Blacks at 13.9 percent. The city has now gained a reputation among the other suburbs of Toronto as an ethnic enclave, just like Richmond Hill for Asians and Vaughan for Italians. You can read visible discomfort on the faces of non-Indian people as they gaze upon strip malls with Hindi signs.

Neighbourhood conspiracy theories circulate about how South Asians are getting money to buy all the new developments in Brampton, about how they are "taking over" the government. That rhetoric of ethnic groups "taking over" historically precedes the reassertion of white dominance.

In Brampton, we witness the irony—or is it hypocrisy?—of white inclusive policies. White policy-makers congratulate themselves on the majority presence of a single non-white group. The presence of Indians in Brampton means that the area is diverse. Checkmark. Move on. In this way, the diversity of an area causes the white imagination to dismiss the area. Move out. Diversity to them means difference *between* groups. What white people rarely address is the incredible diversity *within* a group. A Black area comprises Somalis and Ethiopians and Ghanaians and Jamaicans and Haitians and descendants of Black Canadian slaves, etc. Same with South Asians. The Indians in Brampton are not all Indian by nationality, but Sri Lankan or Pakistani or Bangladeshi. The signs on the strip malls may not be Hindi but Urdu. The language we hear around us is more likely languages, plural. Within the Indian diaspora, people can prefer other identities: Sikh or Punjabi or Gujarati or Bengali or Brahmin.

My parents did not move out of Brampton. I'm there often. We are not a part of the majority group in the city. We were never. I can imagine what white nostalgia feels like. One sees businesses opening and closing according to the desires of the rising community, but not yours. Exclusion. Displacement. At the worst of times, people knock on my mother's door to ask if she'd like to sell her house. Communication is occasionally difficult with older South Asian people. But that's where my foray into empathy ends. I actually don't resent South Asians for transforming the landscape of my childhood. I don't grieve. I still feel free to wander the malls, to patronize the same post office my family has for decades, even if it is under new management. I see a community that is not organized by whiteness, that is unapologetically present, that inhabits the buildings, colleges, and schools built by others as if they always belonged there. I see young people flirting in the streets, new immigrants waiting on the bus to deliver them to an overnight shift, old men on park benches leaning on canes. They have formed friendships late in life, so far away from where they started. Did they consider this life for themselves when they were young, handsome, and tall in Punjab?

When I walked with Chiayi through our neighbourhood in Vancouver, people seemed to relax. She would stop in front of houses and take pictures of people's gardens. I stood on the sidewalk, scanning the street. No one gave her looks for taking photos of their lilacs. She would ask homeowners about their coyote squash and wisteria. They offered us grapes from their vines. Such things never happen when I am alone. I am aware of the kind of privilege and access that her race grants me.

Once, when we were walking, I stopped in front of a house I admired and a man came out. I saw that, when he noticed me, something in him rose, like a tinted car window, like he thought I might return later and rob his house. But when he saw Chiayi, the window rolled down. He told us that he built the house himself. He told us about the architect. I listened politely. I tried to visibly admire his house, but not too much.

In Vancouver, there is a similar fear of Asians taking over, not so much the city's civic life but its real estate. Headlines: RACE AND REAL ESTATE: HOW HOT CHINESE MONEY IS MAKING VANCOUVER UNLIVABLE; IMMIGRATION HAS "UNDOUBTEDLY" ESCALATED HOUSING PRICES IN VANCOUVER, TORONTO, SAYS STUDY; VANCOUVER HAS BEEN TRANSFORMED BY CHINESE IMMIGRANTS; DOES CHINA'S MONEY THREATEN CANADA'S SOVEREIGNTY?; IS YOUR CITY BEING SOLD OFF TO GLOBAL ELITES?

Like the Greater Toronto Area, the Greater Vancouver Area also has its ethnic enclaves. The city becomes more diverse as you travel east. Affluent white and Asian people live in Point Grey. I lived near Little India. As you go east and south beyond the city, you'll find large Chinese populations in Burnaby and Richmond (53 percent) and South Asians in Surrey (32 percent).

Vancouver is more conspicuously moneyed than Toronto. BMWs are Vancouver's Honda. It's no big deal to see Porsches, Ferraris, Lamborghinis, Aston Martins. Students traverse campuses in Balenciaga and Supreme. They carry boxy Fjällräven backpacks. They step on the backs of their Gucci shoes until they're flattened into a pair of slippers. At minimum wage, those shoes cost two weeks of work. Two of Canada's three most profitable malls are in Vancouver. Near Pacific Mall, in the city's luxury zone, there are stores so fancy I have never heard of them, but I know they're not for me. (How do you know that? Why are you limiting yourself? Please. Let's not kid ourselves.)

Allow me a hypothesis. I'm fine if it's proven wrong. I can't help but think the extreme valuation and conspicuous consumption in Vancouver is a display of people proving they are worth being here. The policies of immigration attract the best people of a foreign country—more points for doctors, graduate degrees, etc.—then question their credentials, then underemploy and devalue them with stunning systemic biases. I don't know how many generations it takes to get beyond that debasement. And so, to compensate, the immigrants to Vancouver (those who can) buy expensive properties, things, so all you see upon looking at them is their value, taken to a literal extreme. Not all. Some of the money is old money, built over generations in Canada, and held quietly. Some of the money is relocated money, perhaps from Hong Kong into Canadian investments in the event that political tensions with mainland China escalate. Some of the money is young money, spent as if the world were a playground. Again, of course, there are Asians in Vancouver for whom none of this is true. Yet how are they perceived? I wonder if all of the money associated with Asians in the region looks equally threatening to white Canadians who see no way to compete with it. Hence the headlines.

* * *

In Vancouver, at the University of British Columbia, I

gave my (mostly white) students an exercise designed to increase their capacity for risk and empathy. The exercise goes like this: Visit a place that makes you uncomfortable or insecure. If you grew up in a city, go into a forest, into the wild (safely, etc.), veer off path (safely, etc.), encounter the terror of aporia. If you are from a suburb, venture into the poorest postal code in Canada, East Hastings. Don't rush through. Find a place to be and stay there. Don't ignore people. Write there without anthropologizing or trafficking in misfortune. Note your anxieties. As a third option, I suggest entering an upscale store where you don't think you'd be welcome. Process the experience and allow yourself to be processed.

One fall, I did that last version of the assignment. I went into an expensive store in Vancouver's luxury zone with a friend, a Brown guy, born and raised in a very white Quebec town. My friend was expensively dressed, as usual. See the above hypothesis. The salesperson was friendly. He followed us upstairs. We were not harassed. In my head, I heard the white chorus say, See, we told you so. You've been a presumptuous, paranoid dick. The problem is with you, not us.

Would I ever go back to that store again? No. Why? Beyond the evidence of this experience, I know that I am not the desired client in that space. It cannot be proven. It can only be known.

The exercise that I would like to give students involves asking them to go into a place where they are the only person of their race and attempt an interaction without using any of their privileges, of whiteness, of gender, of money. As a minority in that situation, divested of power, how do you even begin to engage with an impervious world? Like Prufrock, when you are pinned and wriggling on the wall, then how would you begin?

KOREA: FOREIGN BODY

There once was a little boy named Amir, my partner tells me. He was in an after-school programme created to keep kids off the Chicago streets. The programme was run by earnest white people and staffed by college students, like my partner, trying to make tuition money.

One day, she stood over Amir's desk as he was drawing. She was careful not to compliment his work because he had a habit of destroying whatever art the adults praised.

Without lifting his eyes from the page, he asked, Are you Chinese?

She was taken aback by the question. He had seen her every school day since the programme began. Was it a blanket question about whether all Asians were Chinese? Or was it the opposite, an attempt to precisely locate her ethnic roots within the Asian diaspora? Chiayi is not Chinese. She is Taiwanese. It's a point she insists on with adults. But with little Amir, she was unsure how to respond. Nearby children tuned in for her answer.

Amir answered before she could. He said, *I'm* Chinese.

No you're not, said one of his friends.

Shut up, Amir said. You don't know what being Chinese means.

In the title story of my short story collection *Not Any-one's Anything*, I write from the point of view of a Korean student. She resists the advances of a Serbian grad student, a real chameleon, who tries on identities and discards them. It's the kind of identity-fluid story one could write unmolested a decade ago.

Recently, in an interview about appropriation, that story came up. The interviewer asked, "Did the idea of potentially crossing acceptable boundaries—in taking stories or voices—enter your thinking as part of the process?" It's the kind of question where you see a bear trap opening over your career.

I acknowledged the obvious, that I was neither female nor Korean. I noted that I had lived in Korea for a while. I pointed to years of Korean language classes as evidence of my process before writing that story. I talked about embodied research. I admitted that no amount of research could get right to the soul of someone else. We devalue people when we assume that we know them fully. I didn't mention that the story is all about identity shifting, but apart from that, I made the points I wanted to make.

Still, the lie at the heart of fiction, of an author becoming someone else in a story that is not his own, will forever remain unresolved. What made me think I could write credibly as a Korean woman? Should I shut up? Do I know what being Korean means?

In Korea, I was relatively unbothered by my status as a 외국 사람 or foreign person, outsider, literally other country person. See, I still want to impress you with my Korean.

Although I was conspicuous by race and language, I was nevertheless handled with care. I'm not naive. My basic humanity did not prompt the effusion of Korean hospitality. Everyone knew I was there temporarily to teach English. The private education industry in Korea is valued at US $17 billion. English institutes alone account for $5 billion. Apart from that one skill with my tongue, I would make no meaningful impact on the country. The kindness of Koreans had more to do with cultural norms than with a verdict about the worth of my humanity.

At the English institute where I worked, the adult students could be housewives or businessmen. It was in Korea that I first made a point I would often repeat in the future. *Your English ability has nothing to do with your intelligence. The fact that you can't express yourself doesn't mean that you don't have thoughts to express.* Some people appreciated that validation. Some university students came to the institute to improve their TOEFL scores, or as a reintroduction to education after military service, or to prepare for the job market. Some were under a spell that English would make them happier. The school-age students were overworked, overstuffed with knowledge, visibly fatigued—the institute one stop among many on an after-school educational circuit designed to make them competitive in the future. To meet all these needs, classes ran from six in the morning to ten or eleven at night.

Many Koreans I encountered had an almost infantile fascination with difference. White instructors basked and racialized instructors bristled under the Korean curiosity about our hair, skin, jawline, neck length, you name it.

Random people on the street would ask me, Where are you from? I made them guess. Africa, the children guessed. America, the university students guessed. Or hoped. Nobody ever guessed Canada.

I am altogether too forgiving about this sort of thing. Even now, I understand that the inquisitors were partly placing my skin and partly placing my accent. Accents aren't readily apparent if one is still learning a language. I was a vessel of a certain kind of English and students wanted to know where each vessel was made. To be sure, they preferred white teachers. They associate America and Canada with white natives, not Indigenous or any other race, and so the purest form of English should come from the white body. The institute that I worked for—and many others—limited its teachers to citizens of the US, Canada, the UK, Australia, and South Africa. You better hold one of those passports. Teachers from the Philippines were second-class. Native English speakers who were Asian-Canadian or Asian-American were made to answer many more questions to prove their English authenticity.

Among the foreign teachers, there were sometimes squabbles. In one city, I taught among South Africans—one white, one Black. The white South African was civil to me, and a chillier level of civil to the Black South African. I can recall his face. Tightness near the lips. This evidence would not be valid in a court of law, yet the white one looked at the Black one with disapproval, meant to be invisible but nonetheless readable by any Black person. Why such contempt? I'd guess that the Black South African equally represented their home country to these

Koreans. The white South African had the breezy, adventurous ease of a life of whiteness and mountain air. The Black one was in Korea for the money more than the experience. He maintained his cheerfulness in spite of the white one. There they both were, struggling to uphold or abolish apartheid in a country where they were both conferred equal footing yet were both in the minority.

AMERICA: BODY DOUBLE

Chiayi and I met at a job interview in Indiana. The university was staging some sort of initiative to diversify their non-diverse faculty with diverse people of diversely diverse diversity. In this manner, the university sold itself to us. We sold ourselves to it. Chiayi and I wore black and snuck looks at each other through the rain. Neither of us got jobs there.

Ten years later, we were in Vancouver, putting on our sneakers to go running, and I asked her a question I should have asked her when we met in Indiana.

Have you ever had a Black prof?

She scrolled through her memory. No, she said.

How about a Black teacher?

Definitely not, she said. She grew up in a small Midwestern town that was 94 percent white, a census number she argues is a gross underrepresentation of its whiteness.

Have you ever had a teacher or professor who was not white?

Nope.

I paused to consider the implications of this thoroughly white education, given that we both work within universities.

No, wait, she said. My Japanese instructor was Japanese. She wasn't a professor, though.

I clarified: I don't mean language teachers. My Korean prof was Korean.

Then no.

We stood up, ready to leave the condo.

There was one Asian professor who taught computer science, she said.

It felt like a victory, albeit a bit of a stereotype. Chiayi's brother is a math teacher, by the way.

I never had class with her, Chiayi said.

A few days later, I found her at her laptop, scrolling through the faculty of the institutions she attended for confirmation.

Not one, she said to no one in particular.

I am the only Black professor some of my students will ever have. Occasionally, they remind me that I am a novelty.

At the beginning of my teaching career, students in my composition class were completing course evaluations around the time of the Great American Boycott of 2006. Immigrants, led by Latinx people, planned to withdraw from work, school, and commerce on May 1 in protest of proposed reforms to immigration laws. I absented myself from the room, as college policy goes, while students completed the evaluations, but from the outside I could hear them—all white—buzzing in debate over the boycott. By the time I was signalled in, the buzz had grown to a roar, and the students weren't so much debating as trading clichés about immigrants. They seemed to have reached consensus, more or less. One particularly vocal student saw me in the doorway, realized his opportunity, and struck: Dr. Williams, you can come in now. We have your green card ready.

What followed was the kind of laughter and wincing that comes when someone gets roasted. Too slow to react, I played the part of a good sport. This class was one of my favourites that semester. The students were frank and open to identifying and interrogating their biases. Yet, in that moment, I felt my status slip away, the way it did whenever I left my role as professor or writer and became simply a Black man in America. Suddenly the classroom had become a politicized nation, patrolled by student-officers who were bound in solidarity as Americans. And I, literally stepping in from the outside hallway, had become the immigrant.

Later, walking back to my office, I processed that bout of disorientation. Why didn't I defend myself? Why didn't I say, at the very least, That joke is inappropriate? Why did I find my resources as Herr Dr. Professor Williams, PhD, bankrupt at that moment?

I remembered where I was: a dying mill town making perennial efforts at revitalization. Upon arrival at the train station, one beheld destitute people trying to stay warm inside a Dunkin' Donuts. According to the 2010 US census, the town was 78 percent white, 5 percent Black, 4 percent Asian, less than 1 percent Native American, 4 percent multiracial, and 9 percent other. Among these groups, 21 percent also identified as Latinx. (Wherever I live, I'm interested in such numbers.) The university was the major employer. It was integrated into a residential part of the city yet segregated from the residents; that is, the racialized people who lived in the surrounding streets never walked through campus.

The university itself was predictable in its composition. There were no Black people in senior administrative positions. Black professors were concentrated in the sociology department. Racism in academic circles tends to be subdued and systemic rather than direct and interpersonal. It occurs in the insistent invisibility of whiteness. In seven years, I taught fewer than seven Black students.

Racialized people of my generation know what it's like to be educated more or less exclusively by white people. I survived that. Now I wonder what happens to racialized people who teach predominantly white classes year after year. Every time we look into our classes, we are aware that people like us are missing. There's nobody to fact-check our existence. Instead, we're checked against a series of stereotypes.

The usual inferiority issues smouldered in me that would in any young professor, not even a year out of grad school, in his first tenure-track job. What was I but an affable guy, awfully miscast as a professor? To be harder on myself, my identities not only undermined my claim to the position but rendered me forever unable to be good at my job. I was, after all, a Canadian teaching American literature to Americans, a Caribbean Black man teaching African-American literature, again, to Americans. I received my credentials by studying literature but my credibility by passing as (African-)American in class. When convenient or necessary, the closeness of my ethnicity and geography to the assumed American standard could be substituted for authenticity. Black is Black. Canada's close enough.

The official course evaluations were mercifully uneventful, considering that professors of colour are routinely rated lower on such evaluations. Or maybe I've blacked them out. The only comment I remember from my first year of teaching—from all my years teaching in the US, in fact—was posted on RateMyProfessor.com, that paragon of dispassionate commentary (comment since "red-flagged" and removed): "Liberal Canadian snob."

The need that foreign professors feel to pass in America, to melt in the pot, exhibits itself in anxiety over teaching, because the skin, the hair, the accent, the hijab that is concealed in scholarly writing becomes undeniably apparent when we stand before a class.

In response, a racialized professor might find herself stripping words down to Latin etymology to show mastery of English (seen it) or marking severely to suggest higher standards than other professors (seen it, done it). A POC of a different temperament might become passive, frustrated, nervous, or terse in front of his classes. Teaching becomes a draining performance of composure; office hours interminable stretches of holding one's ground while appearing accommodating.

When it comes to nationality, as a Canadian in America,

an identity that is not as apparent as being British or Indian, say, I have heard my share of hockey and igloo jokes, seal hunting even, some of which I genuinely find funny. But I didn't find *liberal Canadian snob* funny. Whatever mild political view I held remained outside the classroom at the time. Even during what should have been a contentious classroom debate on immigration, I mainly strove to trouble unexamined media regurgitations. After checking the date of the entry, I surmised that the student was displeased with a recently returned essay.

Sorry to keep dwelling on this. I really shouldn't fixate on a little negative comment among generally positive ones, especially when other professors, who cannot pass as American, receive even more hostile comments because of their accents, as if American pronunciation were a measure of intelligence. I refer again to RateMyProfessor.com: "Horrible teacher. Did not speak English too well;" "He is hard to understand due to his thick accent and it hurts to listen;" "She is the worst teacher ever! her accent is hard to understand;" "Hard to understand at first, and gets a little nervous in front of the class;" and so on. For English professors especially, in North American society, where oral communication, not writing, is the measure of authority and authenticity, the inability to speak in cadence raises doubt as to whether the professor has anything of value to say at all.

Convincing students that they have something to learn about composition or the mechanics of language from someone who looks like me and "misspells" *colour* and "mispronounces" *about*, to use cute examples, is an issue not automatically faced by American speakers. Though

Canadian English is "close enough," I still heard an insinu-
ation of doubt regarding my claim to the language when a
student asked, You guys, like, speak French up there, right?

Chiayi set her laptop in front of me.

Look what I found, she said.

Onscreen, there was a Black man, smiling and wearing a tie.

Who's this? I asked.

The library school hired a Black professor.

I scroll down the screen. He's the only Black face
among fourteen.

Welcome. I'm your professor for Nineteenth-Century
African-American Literature, Ian Williams. I'm not actually African-American.

The American students smile. They titter. They
exchange looks, unsure what's going on. Then I try to clar-
ify. It takes longer than you'd expect.

I'm Black, I say. Canadian.

Some light bulbs go on. Some stay off.

Yeah, someone says, but you're still African-American.

That's the moment that I'm prepared for. Many white
students don't see the term African-American as being a
national designator. It's a term that applies to all Black people whether we are American or not. So point number 1 in
class with Americans, who are prepared to talk about race
to some degree, is to expand the notion of Blackness
beyond America, then beyond Africa.

For a Canadian to pass as an American is easy enough. Our accents, our mannerisms, our cultures are similar; our motivations are explained by similar theories, whether those be capitalism, Judeo-Christianity, evolutionary biology, or Freud. By comparison, anxiety about being a Black man who passes as an African-American seems self-inflicted, an almost unnecessary conundrum. Yet being Black is not the same as being African-American. African-American is a brand of Blackness so popular, powerful, and performable that it relegates other diasporic brands to the negligible cultural margin. Even next to unhyphenated Africanism, African-Americanism stands as the imperial brand referenced most easily as the stereo/prototype of Blackness.

Passing implies a hierarchy. One passes for inclusion into a group above one's own. I'd be deceiving myself if I believed that the class joker was well-intentioned as he offered an invitation to become part of the hegemonic group, albeit on conditions that preserve my otherness. *Dr. Williams, you can come in now. We have your green card ready.* I feel the condescension in his comment, premised on his sense of entitlement as a middle-class, white American man. Between us, age and educational disparity disappeared. Being American trumps all other identity markers.

In order to pass in my role as a credible professor of African-American literature, I became African-*American*. I'd go as far as saying that every person of African descent in America becomes African-American regardless of association with Africa or the Caribbean or Britain or Canada. Thus, the history of African-Americans became mine by virtue of my skin and my temporary placement within the borders of the country. It's a peculiar feeling, this general-ization that claimed me; none of my white American col-leagues would become British in England or Canadian in Canada. American status (I don't mean that legally) is maintained everywhere in the world, unless it's convenient to hide under shared whiteness. Being American trumps all—I already said it.

No surprise, then, that such a universally acceptable brand of being is alluring. Passing as American or African-American does not have to turn one into a race traitor. It can be a temporary convenience. It can destabilize the fixedness of national and ethnic identity by its fluidity. Right. But to be perfectly honest, which means foregoing that contrived, optimistic conclusion, if I exploit at whim my ability to pass as native to Canada, the Caribbean, or America, I am little more than a philanderer, a coward who denies the complexity of his multiple allegiances. Instead of quarrelling with systems archaic and powerful enough to make identity categorical, my passing signals tacit submis-sion. It endorses stratification of those who have power, those who pass for people with power, and those fighting for some.

* * *

I have one body, yet it receives so many reactions. This is true for many racialized people. As Chiayi was getting into a cab in Washington, DC, two drunk politician-looking men leered at her, glanced at me, and made some between-men joke.

My partner and I share an immigrant understanding that other ways of thinking and living are as valid as North American ways. We get smug sometimes at the blind spots of North Americans. The smugness, I think, attempts to elevate our occasional outsider status. We have charged memories of the countries where we were born and the years when white kids made fun of our pronunciation and the categories that people are so intent on filling with our bodies. We know, too, that as kids who were raised here, who pass adoptively, we live on the inside of North American culture in a way our parents do not. Between us, there's an immigrant code that the West is not the centre of humanity. The whole world is livable. People live good lives never having encountered whiteness.

Given our position both inside and outside, it's no surprise that we ended up together. We orbit each other.

SIGHTING

⚓ Vancouver
Sun Oct 18

I am sitting in my car behind a friend's building with my partner. I sight a Black boy. He's alone, about ten years old, wearing green camouflage clothing and a mask. He waits near the rear entrance of a community centre. He reads the sign on the fence. He's hoping that the centre is open. He walks to another entrance. A Black girl with a backpack joins him. His sister? A white man comes, tries his card at the door. It doesn't work. He leaves. The Black children leave. A white woman opens the door from the inside.

Mon Oct 19
5:09 P.M.

While driving, I sight the long brown dreadlocks of a pedestrian. Maybe he's—Is he? No, he is not Black.

5:11 P.M.

A few blocks later, I sight a Black man entering a car. A woman with a surgical mask is strapping a (her? their?) child into the car seat.

6:23 P.M.

I sight a Black woman pushing a white girl in a stroller.

6:30 P.M.

I sight a Black boy waiting on a white man to throw a Frisbee to him. The man sees me walking along the edge of the park. He throws the Frisbee to the child and congratulates him loudly for catching it.

Tue Oct 20

On my way to the dentist, I see a Black man mowing a tiny patch of grass on city property. I think the words *invisible labour.*

Wed Oct 21
White rain.

Thu Oct 22

On Zoom, students return to the main room after I close a breakout room. A Black face flickers, but before I can process it, the student turns off his camera and disappears into the 120 students in the class. A Black woman, same—a flicker before she disappears—but she has a photo of herself as her Zoom profile tile.

Fri Oct 23
White rain.

Sat Oct 24

I count eight Black people at church. It's the only time

I see a critical mass of Black people each week. Sister Alma is back from knee surgery. Her husband is celebrating his eightieth birthday. The only Black woman around my age is back for the first time since the first COVID lockdown. She is keeping her hair natural. The pastor's son has not cut his hair in months either. His box cut slopes outward from his head like Nefertiti's crown.

Sun Oct 25
I am driving south on Main Street. A Black woman waits to cross the street outside a Tim Hortons. She is wearing snow pants although it is not very cold by Canadian standards. New immigrant? I feel ashamed of the snap assumption.

Mon Oct 26
White rain.

Tue Oct 27
The automatic doors of the Save-On-Foods part to reveal a Black security guard. I head-nod. He smiles under his mask. After I check out, I see him enter the dollar store in the mall, still in uniform. He pauses in front of the soda fridges. Something has changed in his movements. He seems more relaxed. No, not relaxed. Submissive. I wonder what drink he will buy there that he wouldn't buy at the expensive store he protects and who, apart from me, is watching him.

Wed Oct 28
White rain.

Thu Oct 29
4:09 P.M.

I think I see a Black man inside the U-Haul storage office. In reality, he is actually a life-sized cardboard cutout of a U-Haul employee.

4:28 P.M.

I go to the Vancouver dump to dispose of old building materials. It's a dark, foul, indoor place. I back my car up to the edge of the pit and toss baseboard and flooring scraps into Jabba. I place a bucket near the edge.

What's in the bucket? an employee asks.

It's drywall compound. I read part of the label to him. It keeps the dust down when you're sanding.

You can't dump that here.

No?

Seeing my confusion, he lowers his mask. He is Black. He says, There's a place on Ontario and 69th. You can take it there.

At Ontario and 69th, I meet a Middle Eastern man.

We don't take that here, he says.

I was sent here, I say.

Well, we don't accept it.

Where does?

Dunno.

Can I ask someone else?

I'm the manager, he says.

I look around. No one is close enough to intervene. I ask, Where would you go if you were me?

The dump, he says.

I drive home between two questions: Which of these two men is lying? Which of these two men would a white person believe?

Fri Oct 30

Movers arrive. One of them is gregarious and upbeat, nearly evangelical, in a manner I associate with successful twelve-step recovery.

He asks, What do you do for a living?

I respond, What do you think I do?

Some kind of office job, he says.

I'm a professor, I say.

Oh, good for you, he says. I never would have guessed that.

He then tells me stories about "Indians" who broke into his moving truck in northern Ontario and stole a TV. Then about an "Oriental" man who went surfing for the first time in Hawaii, caught a massive wave, got tossed, and landed right back on his board like a ninja. Chiayi is in the bedroom on a Zoom work call, missing this. I don't update his terms. I know I should, but I want my furniture to arrive undamaged. He happily takes all of my things away.

Sat Oct 31. Halloween.

Chiayi and I take the ferry from Vancouver to Victoria. I think I see a Black person on the deck taking photos of the wake of the vessel in the ocean, but no, not Black, he's only styled Black. We walk around the ferry, inside, outside. No one like me.

🦮 Victoria

Sun Nov 1. Daylight savings

My partner discovers this list of Black people on my phone. It's called *Ian's List of Comforts.*

Very creepy, she says. What would you say if a white person kept a list of Black people?

They already do, I say.

Not as comfort, she says.

11:35 A.M.

I pick my feet up as if I have stepped in gum. I have stepped on a Black face. It is part of a mural painted in a public square. The mural says, MORE JUSTICE MORE PEACE. As I am looking, a white cameraman approaches me.

I'm with CTV News, he says. We're looking for a comment about the incident that happened here.

The bear trap yawns.

I say, I can't comment on something I don't know about.

The mural was defaced recently, he explains. He points to the *S* of JUSTICE. This section here was about defunding the police. Some witnesses saw a man with a helmet come by and spray-paint over it.

A white man? I say.

Yes, the cameraman says. Do you have any reactions you'd like to share?

I say, That was my reaction.

Later, Chiayi asks, What do you think that reporter wanted?

You heard him. You were there, I say.

Right, yeah. He didn't approach anyone else for comment, though. Just you.

12:27 P.M.

I say, Do you think we'll see a Black person today?

She says, Today you might have to look in the mirror. Then she imitates my voice: Hey, buddy. I'm so happy to see you.

4:24 P.M.

Chiayi and I hike up a mountain at sunset. At the top is a white man and a tree. Before we can take in the full view of the surrounding mountains, the lake below, before I can use the word *nestled*, the white man starts talking to us. He is holding a beer. He knows everything about everything. Behind him, in the distance, a Black man emerges. We squint at each other. He toasts me with his water bottle. I toast him back. He sits down behind a ridge, hidden from sight. I can only see cigarette smoke rising from where he is. I turn my attention back to the white man, who has not stopped talking. He is explaining the bark of the arbutus tree, which is shedding to reveal new brown bark below. Peels right off, he says. Like skin.

Mon Nov 2
White rain.

Tue Nov 3. Election Day
White reign.

Wed Nov 4
White rain.

Thu Nov 5
White rain.

Fri Nov 6
White rain.

Sat Nov 7
On the ferry from Victoria to Vancouver, a Black teenager sits alone at a table with a bag of fast food in front of him. He eats some of his meal and wraps up the rest for later.

A tall, thin man who wears a bandana in place of a mask considers the menu of the cafeteria then leaves.

A middle-aged man scrolls through his phone. The pace of his scrolling suggests that he's looking for someone to call.

I sight a family. A husband and wife try to feed their squirmy, distracted children. Seeing the woman and the two daughters makes me wonder, Where are the Black women in this province?

⚓ Toronto
Sun Nov 8
The flight is full, despite the pandemic. One of the flight attendants is Black. She's extremely courteous, like

flight attendants from the eighties. Maybe she's new to this. I don't search her chest for a name tag because I don't want her to misread me.

I am waiting outside Pearson Airport for public transit. It's 20 degrees Celsius, unseasonably warm for Toronto in November, but I am wearing a puffy coat and several layers because my luggage is maxed out. I bet, no, I worry that people think I'm a new immigrant. I want to be the kind of Black man who never worries about such perceptions. I consider chewing gum aggressively like a jock.

Mon Nov 9
A muscular Black man walks a tiny dog in Liberty Village while talking on his cell. His girlfriend's?

The Black salesman at the car rental place hooks me up with a car in record time. His shirt is too tight for his belly.

Tue Nov 10
Every time I go out now, I sight Black people.

I make eye contact with a Black man in a parking lot and his walk turns into a swagger.

A Black woman rides a bicycle with a basket. I am afraid for her.

A man holds his daughter's hand with one hand and pushes the empty stroller with the other.

Wed Nov 11, Remembrance Day

At the bike racks outside FreshCo, closing time, I sight a Black guy and his white girlfriend. It looks like he's breaking up with her from how he hangs his head, won't meet her eye, from her stiff body, her hands in the high pockets of her coat. Beneath her coat, she is still in her FreshCo uniform. They're each waiting for the other to say something.

Thu Nov 12

My partner asks, Are you still recording?

What? I ask, because I wasn't taking video on my phone.

Black people, she says.

She has noticed a change in me, a relaxation.

No, I say.

She says, You have enough. You're in a good place.

Fri Nov 13

While walking to get some daisies for an event at the specific request of the organizer, I sight a Black man with artificial daisies in his cart.

Where did you get those? I ask him.

Dollarama, he says.

We talk for a while. His nose is busted. After busking, he tells me, he was carrying all his stuff on his bike and he tried to ride over a railroad track, but he was going too fast and everything went flying. His nose broke his fall. He says that sentence like a punchline to a joke he's told many times. He has a slight accent. Maybe he's Brazilian. I want to ask him where he's from. I see the blue stitches through his nose. I hurry away. I see myself—a man on a chi-chi mission to buy gerbera daisies at 10 A.M. who wanted to ask him where he's from. How easy it is to become the whiteness one beholds. It's like learning to speak: you don't plan to learn, you just hear these voices around you and join in bit by bit until you're speaking the language of the master's house.

On my way home, I see Daisy man again. He's pulling his cart, guitar on his back, heading to a makeshift tent city on King Street. I am holding real daisies; his are artificial, but bigger and livelier than mine. They chatter spontaneously with the world.

Sat Nov 14

I walk to High Park. I encounter so many Black people that I lose count, so many I lose myself. My eyes overflow with honey. So many I forget to count, so many I forget myself.

Sun Nov 15

Queen Street, late night walk with Chiayi, strong winds. The street is generally deserted. An empty streetcar scrapes by. I see a drunk white-coded woman approaching and I know it's going to be bad from the look she gives me, then us, then me. I think she's going to vomit. I move to the edge of the sidewalk. She leans toward us, trying to block us as we pass.

Buffet, she says to us apparently, which is how my phone auto-corrects N███.

Seeing no reaction, she leans closer and goes for something worse.

Nighter jello, she says, according to the auto-corrected version.

The first word is for me and the second for Chiayi.

We take a side street and head back to the empty condo. I am sorry Chiayi had to see that, but also glad that she sees what random, unprovoked racism looks like from my point of view.

We were having a good day.

Mon Nov 16

I start noticing white people.

I notice the white woman who inches forward into the pedestrian zone in her crossover vehicle. When she sees me about to cross, she inches her way into my space and turns the corner.

The Only

The Look

My grandmother told us, Don't look white people in the eye. I'm not sure where she picked up this advice, but the imperative phrasing makes me think that the consequences of such a transgression would be severe. Not far from her house, on the way to the beach, remain vestiges of slavery: the cocoa house, yellow cocoa groves, great houses, and, in the de-colonial period afterward, a house that still bears the name of the white man who owned most of the land.

In elementary school in Canada, we were taught to look people in the eye when we spoke to them. In Trinidad, eye contact is softer, deferential. To avoid someone's eye is a kindness that allows them to look freely. I don't much like eye contact. All the power dynamics, aggression, and confidence of people who make an effort to hold your eye— *blegh*. As recently as my thirties, I've been called autistic— meant as an insult—for this preference, without any consideration of cultural factors at work. Why the armchair diagnosis, though? I just don't want to be looked at.

* * *

One can't talk about constantly being the only Black person in a room without talking about being looked at. Being the Only means being conspicuous.

In one of my workshop classes, I invite students to introduce themselves without words. The exercise is based on a conceptual piece by Marina Abramović, The Artist Is Present. We sit in two rows, knees almost touching, facing each other for one minute before shifting down the row to the next face.

The first few seconds are skittish. Students try to control their smiles, they adjust their clothing, they straighten their posture, they adjust their gaze to a benign frequency. Eventually, their faces settle into a resting state. A gong sounds internally as they recognize that they are both looking and being looked at, and that how they look at others conveys information about who they think they are. Pronominal confusion intended. Are we not always introducing ourselves in this reverberating way?

I then ask them to write the first poem of the semester: "To See and Be Seen."

Every time I do this exercise, I think of a moment in Chaucer's Canterbury Tales where the Wife of Bath positions herself to see and also be seen by "lusty folk." Medieval optics, itself a restatement of ancient Greek optics, professed that the act of seeing involved emitting a ray from your eye, capturing a small impression of the object or person, and bringing it back to your eye. We can still hear remnants of this thinking in *capture an image* or *feast your eyes.*

That's fine and good if you're the one seeing. Being seen, however, can feel like being consumed. It's not easy being looked at. Women and racialized people understand this keenly. We recognize the invasiveness of eyes before we hear terms such as the *male gaze* and *scopophilia* or encounter Foucault's panopticon. White men look, everyone else is looked at.

In university, coming to an awareness of new terms, I wanted to ask two very personal questions: How can I avoid the inevitability of being looked at when I am the only one of my kind in every situation? And if I must be viewed, then how can I be viewed as everyone else is viewed? But these questions had no relevance to other people in the class.

Time for a commercial break.

It begins with an overhead shot of a Black man opening his eyes in bed. The rest of the commercial records the looks he receives as he goes about his day. Sometimes it's shot from his point of view so the looks are directed at us, the viewers. An elevator of white people closes on him/us/you. At a diner, a white couple chooses not to sit in his/our/your area. At a pool, white kids exit as he teaches his son how to float. At an upscale store, salespeople exchange looks when he strolls through. The looks have various nuances—disgust, worry, condescension—but as a cluster, I'd describe them as *degrees of concern.*

At the end of the commercial, the man enters a courtroom. Everyone stands. Turns out he's a judge. The moral: shame on everyone in the commercial. Shame on the viewer too, for being mildly surprised that the Black man has such a good job. Shame, on all y'all. Shame, shame, shame.

Many of the comments on YouTube are from posters who found the commercial moving. A few viewers thought Procter & Gamble missed the mark, that a Black man should not have to be extraordinary, a judge, to be looked at with respect. Fair point.

I recognize the Look he receives because I see it a lot, almost daily. However, when I'm with white people, the Look is negligible, maybe even invisible, to them. I read the Look as racialized; they read it as neutral, as looking rather than a look, as a fellow human scanning their environment. These white people are not insensitive to nuance. If there's something flirtatious or sexual in a look, they pick up on it. So I wonder whether they actually do not see the racialized Look or whether they are denying it in order to avoid a pending race conversation they see as unnecessary. A long, awkward conversation after a quick look.

I'm thinking about my grandmother's advice again. Perhaps she gave it not in order to pay deference to white people but because she was trying to shield us from being objectified, from measuring ourselves through the looks of white people.

If the world keeps looking at you in these minimizing ways, communicating with you non-verbally (famous stat: 70 to 93 percent of communication is non-verbal), one of three things happens.

Either A) you come to view yourself similarly, which begets self-loathing.

B) You confront the viewer: What's your problem? This option gets exhausting. It produces more bad looks, because once you go verbal, you become the aggressor.

Or C) You look away. But you die inside. Your courage shrivels. At best, you retreat into the imagination.

None of these are great options or universally appropriate to every situation. I've mostly done the third with strangers. I can't stop the looks. The only way I can stop the looks is by not looking myself.

AT SCHOOL

In high school, there were two Black tables in the corner of the cafeteria, near the canteen. You didn't sit there unless you were Black, and even if you were, you didn't sit there unless you were invited. The tables were largely ignored but generally the most fun tables in the cafeteria.

I recognized people at the Black tables because there were so few Black people at that school. It was an arts high school in a town called Caledon, which is on the outskirts of Brampton, which is on the outskirts of Toronto. Because the school was in a rural location and admission was by audition, which may have been a gatekeeping mechanism, the student body was very, very white; this deterred many Black folks from attending the school.

I was the only Black guy in the group I hung around with. I did not eat lunch at the Black tables. My friends still asked me about the tables, as if I had special psychic insight into the conversations there. White folks get curious or downright concerned when Black folks congregate. Truth is, I was also curious about what happened there. Imagine a group of Black artsy kids at two alienated tables in a sea of white cafeteria noise, and me, a Black teenager separate from them, like a diasporic island from Africa.

Did I want to join? Did I view them as a kind of ghetto? Did I want to row my raft to their country? No visa arrived, I could say. No application was made, they could say.

However you look at it, I was the Only. The only Black in my friend group. One of the only Blacks in Visual Arts in my grade (I should consult my yearbooks). There was one girl in the grade below me, who left after a year and went to a more diverse school. In almost every one of my classes in high school, I was the only Black kid. In university, I was the only Black kid in my English classes. Every single English course. In big lecture courses for psych or science, I'd sometimes encounter my friend from church and maybe one or two other Black people, whose attendance we both tracked throughout the semester.

I can keep going. I have been the only Black person on a train, the only one in an audience, the only one in a hallway of offices, the only one in countless rooms. Here's yet another way that race structures our lives: the cost of choosing a path that leads you through elite schools and respected jobs is lifelong alienation. You become a kind of Black person who is kind of Black.

Being the Only can be branded as an achievement, as exceptionalism (in both senses), as an example to the race, as a condemnation of others in the race, as a data point. But the experience of being the Only is *felt* mostly as loneliness.

Exceptionalism and achievement are linked in the minds of Black and white people alike. With that achievement comes responsibility. Du Bois believes the Talented Tenth of Black people would "guide the Mass away from the contamination and death of the Worst." Being the Only is often reflected back to you as if it were a privilege for Black people merely to be in the presence of white people.

The whiter the environment, the more you've achieved. Said differently, the fewer Black people in that environment, the more you've achieved. Sometimes the Only coincides with being the First. The First is slippery because it slides from marking you as the first Black person in time to gain admission, say, to the first in position. The best.

So I was the Only in my class. What do I want? A medal? Pity? Why is it important not to be alone in a lecture hall? Was anyone jeering at me? Wasn't everyone there to learn? These are white questions.

If you're white, reverse the situation: imagine yourself as the only white person in a teeming cafeteria of Black people, all with their various temperaments, subjectivities, energies, not just for one meal but for four years of lunches. Now imagine two white tables in the corner. Most white people would join. I reckon most white people (or their parents) wouldn't stay in that situation.

The very endurance and patience of Black people in outlier situations, conspicuous and marginal as a means to an end, sure, but also as a reality of our day-to-day existence, means that we are not short-sighted or quick-tempered or violent, as popular stereotype would hold. Quite the opposite. We are long-suffering.

Earlier, I mentioned the scholar Christina Sharpe, who describes anti-Black racism as weather, as the atmosphere we live in. I think about it in similarly environmental terms. Racism is like radiation: sometimes it is low-grade like cell-phone signals, sometimes intense like a nuclear explosion. Whatever the degree, its effects accumulate. It's not an environment that harms Black people alone. White people can be radioactive.

I'm looking at my high school yearbooks and my university graduation class photo to see if Black people were, in fact, as rare as I recall.

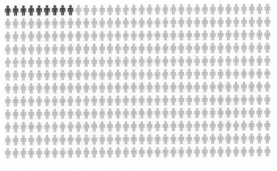

Grade 10   ● Black   ● Non-Black

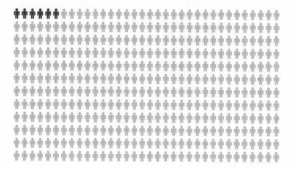

Grade 11 ● Black ● Non-Black

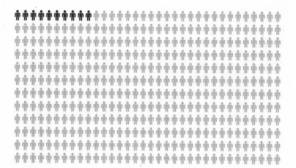

Grade 12 ● Black ● Non-Black

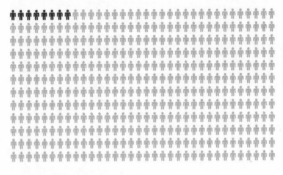

University graduating class ● Black ○ Non-Black

AT WORK

Auntie Verna worked as a nurse in England for most of my childhood. In the eighties, she was part of a team that delivered a premature baby so small she fit in her father's palm. The event was commemorated in a British newspaper, and my mother saved the clipping in the album alongside photographs of Auntie Verna walking through snow, Auntie Verna in a fur coat, Auntie Verna with her hair pulled back into a bun.

Our family had the usual fascination with the clipping. There was pride in her achievement and its recognition. To be in the newspaper, in print, was a big deal. But the article also caused gentle head shaking. We found the headline amusing: thanks a bundle, girls! And we found the photograph bemusing. Here was Auntie Verna, the only Black nurse in the photograph, shoulder to shoulder with three white nurses and the baby's mother. She is looking at the white baby in front of her with the most reserved smile of all the nurses. If I cover the smiles with my thumb and look into the eyes of everyone, I sense all sorts of dynamics behind the scenes. Auntie Verna's Trinidadian relatives admitted pride in her accomplishment. They could even admit a parallel pride in the fact that she was in the newspaper. But below that was an unspeakable pride that Auntie Verna was surrounded by white people.

In all the places I've taught over the last fifteen years, I've only had three Black colleagues in my department. Okay, one was not in my department, but our offices were on the same floor. So, two. And one was precariously employed as a sessional. So, in all the places I've taught, I've only had one tenure-stream Black colleague in my department.

It was a job that I wasn't on track to get. I went on the market ABD (that is, all-but-dissertation), sent out fifty applications, each requiring an assortment of materials and follow-up diversity forms. I made it to a couple of long lists and had a whopping one interview. Back then, the annual convention of the Modern Language Association (MLA) was where universities interviewed candidates before selecting a short list to invite to campus. It was an elimination round. The bathrooms and hallways bristled with black-suited PhDs, all in competition, mumbling dissertation synopses to themselves. Everybody's dissertation was *problematizing* something or other. A friend's toenails fell off from the stress.

Early in my interview, which took place on a hotel bed in Philadelphia, I knew I wasn't going to get the job. At first sight, I was not the candidate they were looking for. I could tell from the polite procedural efficiency of the interviewers that they were not really listening to me. They looked at their papers. They waited for me to finish. We shook hands.

They said: Thank you for your time.

They couldn't say: This was a waste of time.

They would never say: You are not what we're looking for, Black man.

But I still needed a job. So I went down to the large convention room to look at open postings. The room was like the Walmart of academia. Rows and rows of universities, interviewing candidates at folding tables. I decided to browse along the aisles since I was already wearing my suit and had my materials on me. Most schools were in the middle of interviews. I saw a Black man and a white woman with no candidate in front of them. I recognized the name of the university. I had applied there, I told them, but I didn't get a call back.

The Black man said, You're here now.

The white woman said, What's your name?

And the Black man said, Tell us about yourself.

Emotionally, it was like a sea of ice breaking up. I gave them my CV. We talked right there and then. Every time someone approached the table, I looked over my shoulder and prepared to leave. They assured me that I was not taking someone else's time. I was who they wanted to speak to right now. And yet they were clear that they had other candidates to meet and were constrained by certain hiring protocols, meaning I should not hope unreasonably. They thanked me when we were done.

About a month later, I got invited for a campus visit, then some time after that I was offered one of two jobs in their department. I don't know what kind of advocacy happened behind the scenes because of these two people. Did I get that job because a Black man was on the committee? That's a question that white people ask when they feel disadvantaged. It strips Black people of our qualifications by surrendering us to the favours of Black people or the benevolence of white people. I was qualified. I could do the job as well as other candidates. I did it. I can point to my record. But in competitive processes, I must do the pre-work of Blackness that white people don't need to do, which is the work of persuasion that I am in fact a contender. That work takes the form of being articulate and personable, of being smart, of letting white people know that they are seen, that they matter. And then there's a click inside the white person, a lock unlocking from the other side, and the door opens enough that they can see me and we can finally get down to business. With the Black man, I didn't need to dance on the other side of the door before he opened it.

At that MLA convention in Philadelphia, Toni Morrison was one of the featured presenters. The room was full. I squeezed myself into the back. I was just a boy from Brampton, trying to get a job among glittering people from expensive schools, but she seemed to speak straight to me:

Certain kinds of trauma visited on peoples are so deep, so stupefyingly cruel, that—unlike money, unlike vengeance, even unlike justice, rights, or the good will of others—art alone can translate such trauma and turn sorrow into meaning, sharpening the moral imagination.

If both paths led to the same security, I would have written a novel instead of a dissertation.

I'll confess something. I didn't think I was going to win the Giller because some of the other finalists had been on the list before. They were bridesmaids two or three times; it was their turn. I didn't think I would win because it was my first novel and a challenging one, a multicultural story and the world was swinging back to white supremacy. And, to be honest, I didn't think I was going to win because I was Black. Esi Edugyan, a Black woman, won the year before for the second time, a rare feat. No way would they give the prize to Black folks two years in a row. And André Alexis, a Black man, had won a few years before, so no way, and Madeleine Thien, an Asian woman, before that. The prize was becoming unrecognizably non-white. Canlit wouldn't go Black. Then, the year after me, Souvankham Thammavongsa, a Laotian woman, won. She passed on the advice she lives by: Live as if you've already won.

* * *

Gayatri Chakravorty Spivak was on the same round-table panel as Morrison. In situations where I am hypervisible as the Only and called upon, implicitly, to represent the entire race, as if there is a single Black position on any issue but multiple white positions, I recall Spivak's double bind. Add Black to her identity markers below:

> The question of "speaking *as*" involves a distancing from oneself. The moment I have to think of the ways in which I will speak as an Indian, or as a feminist, the ways in which I will speak as a woman, what I am doing is trying to generalize myself, make myself a representative, trying to distance myself from some kind of inchoate speaking *as such*. [. . .] But when the card-carrying listeners, the hegemonic people, the dominant people, talk about listening to someone "speaking as" something or the other, I think *there* one encounters a problem. When *they* want to hear an Indian speaking as an Indian, a Third World woman speaking as a Third World woman, they cover over the fact of the ignorance that they are allowed to possess, into a kind of homogenization.

It is not fair that one Black person has to represent the race while a room of white people represent only themselves.

In Public

There is no guarantee that Black people are inclined to help each other out. Our interactions are not all head nods and fist bumps. In fact, a Black person can guard the position of the Only to prevent others from achieving a commensurate level of success. It's a disturbing reality, especially in a culture where winning is defined as being the only one to have succeeded. For two Black people socialized into whiteness, beholding each other in a room of greying white administrators, for instance, can be tense. Is she the kind of Black person who hangs out with Black people publicly? Does he think I'm one of those affirmative action brothers? Will I offend them by my presence? Will she think I'm hitting on her?

I used to worry about approaching Black people through the white rain. I understand how much labour went into building the fragile tower of our acceptance. How dare I knock it down by offering my hand?

A few years ago, I spent some time at the Banff Centre for the Arts, working with a team on a documentary/text/dance production. My role was challenged from the outset (insert white man: "Let's be clear about who's running the show") and the entire project never fulfilled its intentions, as far as I know. I did my part and went back to working on my first novel, *Reproduction*.

During that month, I saw no Black people. No artists, no business people, no administrators, no food staff. I didn't notice at first, but the moment I did, I couldn't return to ignorance. My eyes grew hungry for someone like me.

On the evening of the premiere of the dance performance, I was in champagne-flute conversation with a friend when I saw a Black man, wearing a cowboy hat, next to an

Indigenous woman and their baby. I told my friend that I was going to do it, I had to, I was going to say hi. She pretended to release a dove with her hands and off I went through the white rain. I don't remember the conversation with the man. He probably introduced his family. I probably made a joke. He was chill. We don't exchange Christmas cards or anything. And although there was no bond there, I felt better about the world afterward.

I was having lunch with my publisher one day at a swanky place in Toronto. I had been living in Vancouver for a while by that point. Skin hunger was gnawing. The host led a Black man and a white woman, similar dynamic to ours, to a nearby table. I divided my attention. Eventually, I went to the bathroom, then on the way back stopped at his table, interrupted, said I'd been overhearing parts of his conversation, said he reminded me of someone, was he a creative type? Had we met? We tried to superimpose our histories. No overlap. We did not offer each other jobs. But we could not deny a kind of symmetry. He made a card of himself on the napkin and gave it to me. That was all. That was enough. And I felt a world better afterward.

James Baldwin knows about being the Only and the First.
In "Stranger in the Village," he makes a point about the difference between being the first white man to be seen by a Black person and the first Black person to be seen by a white person: "The white man takes the astonishment as tribute, for he arrives to conquer and to convert the natives, whose inferiority in relation to himself is not even

to be questioned; whereas I, without a thought of conquest, find myself among a people whose culture controls me, has even, in a sense, created me."

Both America and Canada are created on white power. That's not inflated rhetoric. I mean that the institutions and priorities that shape both countries have white ideologies at their foundation. The difference between the two is that white Americans and Black Americans have been in each other's hair from the founding of their country and that the major shifts of domestic policy have had to reckon with a large Black presence. There's still a huge attempt to keep the words *American* and *America* white and to hyphenate Black Americans as a category, an offshoot, an accessory of the dominant group. Yet a Black American is understood to be from America and not anywhere else. In Canada, there's still a sense that a Black Canadian is from elsewhere—not Canada. Maybe the Caribbean or Africa. White Canadians keep looking for a source of that Blackness, whereas white Americans know that Black people are as much a historical part of their country as white people are.

All those years that I was surrounded exclusively by white people, I felt myself nipped and tucked, smoothed and eroded, by the contact. I imagine that the North American white person's self-definition functions similarly against the existence of Black people, as if Black people were a fence, holding hands, around their self-concept. Only that fence is electric. In the white imagination, Black people are always charged while white people become charged by contact. Everything outside that fence, all the other fields of unknowability, belongs to Blackness. In the same way that the geocentric Earth relates to space, as the most important point rather than a small and insignificant interruption to the vast darkness, so whiteness positions itself in relation to Blackness.

We could just as easily flip ground and background.

PART 3

THE DRIVE HOME

1.

Pierre and I are driving back to Vancouver from Surrey along a highway that slices through farmland. He's not so much driving as strolling along the highway. It's Saturday afternoon, unpleasantly hot, so we go back and forth between turning on the AC and opening the windows. In the air, there's wildfire smoke, calls for racial justice, and a virus.

Pierre's in good spirits. He tells me that he's been on a staycation for the past two weeks. Didn't look at his e-mail. Sat around eating ice cream and watching Netflix stand-up comedy specials.

A car passes us. The driver looks over at us, annoyed. *Strolling* has become *crawling*. My right foot pushes down reflexively. I'm mildly embarrassed at my role as an accessory to slow driving.

Pierre catches me glancing at the speedometer. He's five kilometres below the speed limit.

Notice how I'm letting everyone pass? he says.

You're giving them a head start, I say.

But he doesn't speed up. A few minutes go by and,

compared with the other cars, it now feels like we're in reverse.

Did you get another ticket or something? I ask.

He takes his eyes off the road to look at me. He seems spooked.

In the time I've known him, he's received tickets for driving through intersections with red-light cameras, for parking in no-parking zones when he used to deliver food to pay for school. Something's different this time.

He says, A cop pulled me over recently.

We both get serious.

I was on my way to meet a client. In Surrey, actually. I was going twenty kilometres over the limit and this cop— he was in a regular car—gave me a ticket.

I wince. That sucks, I say.

Pierre is silent for a while. He is reliving the incident. We are on the same stretch of highway as where he got pulled over.

I know I was going fast, Pierre continues. I was overtaking, so I sped up. Obviously. He snorts. And I looked into the car and I saw his eyes and I knew it was a cop right there and then and that he got me. So he flashes his lights and follows me until we get over the bridge. And that's where I pulled off the road. The cop got out and approached on your side. I saw him walking toward me in the mirror. I put both my hands on the steering wheel like in the movies and he put his hand on his gun. The whole time he was talking to me, he kept his hand on his gun. You know the first thing the cop asked me?

What?

2.

I was in the Vancouver airport on my way to San Francisco for a book event. At the immigration counter, I got sent to the oh-no room. Most of the people in that room were people of colour, including a family where the mother was Middle Eastern and the father was white. The father and two daughters were quickly released, but the mother remained in the holding area with me. As they left, the girls, wearing matching coats, alternately looked back at their mother and up to their father.

When it was my turn, the first thing the white immigration official said to me was not Good morning or Hello, not How are you? or Where are you travelling to today? It was, Have you ever been arrested?

I heard both a question and a threat. The officer detained me for more than ninety minutes. I had to surrender my green card and I missed my flight to San Francisco.

3.

What? I say again. What did he ask you?

"Is this your vehicle?" He thought I stole it.

Pierre drives a 2003 Mercedes-Benz Kompressor. A few days before Christmas one year, we went shopping for cars together in, wow, Surrey again. The car salesman was a caricature of a car salesman whose large head emerged from a low-buttoned shirt. He counted a wad of money on his desk as fast as an automatic money counter. He informed us that the advertised price, the price Pierre was prepared to pay after attempting negotiations, was not the actual price. He wanted another five hundred dollars. I stood behind Pierre, very Papa Bear, and said to him, You can walk away. Just because we drove all the way out here doesn't mean you have to buy it. Pierre, twenty at the time, thought in silence while the salesman and I looked at him. He wanted that car so badly. But he walked away with his four thousand dollars, all the money he had, and bought his Mercedes from someone else.

4.

Whenever I enter my vehicle, I stage a veritable Broadway production. I pull out my keys early. I unlock the door many times with the remote from a distance to signal, Yes, this is my car. I am approaching my car, everybody. I shall enter it forthwith. I stage this production a lot at night and in parking garages. The worst thing would be to reach the door unprepared, fumbling for my keys while white people look at me suspiciously over their shoulders.

When Pierre admitted the same fear, we had a voluble bonding session. No way! You too? He told me about a guy who was rubbernecking him outside his house as he was trying to get into his car, about the time someone broke into his car, smashed the rear quarter window, and thus compelled Pierre to get it fixed immediately so people wouldn't think he was driving a stolen vehicle.

Do our efforts even matter, though?

Weeks after Pierre got pulled over, police in Colorado drew their guns and handcuffed a Black woman and her children. They thought she was driving a stolen vehicle. Turns out it was her car.

In Winnipeg, a man posts on Facebook:

To the "gentleman" who decided that he needed to make me late for work this morning by stopping me to make sure that I was not stealing my own car,

YOU ARE THE PROBLEM, NOT ME!

I can't "move back to where [I] came from"—I was born in this country.

Yes, I'm actually a doctor—I'm glad you were able to read my scrubs.

The other man had blocked his car, then interrogated and insulted him. He assumed the only way this doctor could afford to buy his car was by selling drugs.

In England, Danny Rose, a British soccer player, gives an interview: "I got stopped by the police last week, which is a regular occurrence whenever I go back to Doncaster where I'm from . . . Each time it's, 'Is this car stolen? Where did you get this car from? What are you doing here? Can you prove that you bought this car?'"

5.

I tried to explain to the cop that I was passing, Pierre

says, but he wouldn't give me a chance to talk, so I just kept quiet, and his hand was—you know—the whole time.

By this point in his story, my entire body is tense.

And this cop, he was the standard white boy. Blue eyes, clean-cut. And I was thinking, like, Just tell me what I did and give me the ticket, man.

And meanwhile everyone's passing—

And looking into my car, straight at me, because he's talking to me through the passenger window. And everyone's speeding more than me. And I want to say, Why don't you go after those guys?

Instead, the cop interrogated Pierre. He humiliated him. Humiliation, like shame, does not require an audience. The officer was silencing him and breaking him, not as a spectacle for the people in the passing cars, not even for the officer's own pleasure, not entirely, but simply because he could. Who needs a reason when you're dealing with Black folks? *Why* gives way to *why not.* The officer looked into Pierre's Mercedes and read his demeanour, heard his soft voice, and knew that this kid would compliantly play along to the script. The officer knew that none of the white kids want to play with him. So he played with the Black kid who is under command from society to play. If, out of his uniform and off the job, he had met Pierre, and Pierre had committed a minor social irritation, the word *n██████* might pulse in the officer's head, but he would leave Pierre alone.

I urge the story forward.

So he's interrogating you about all these irrelevant things. He didn't believe I was a designer or that I was going to meet a client. He asked me about that, like, three times. He asked me what I studied in school. He asked me which school. He asked me my immigration status.

Totally irrelevant, I say.

I had already given him my licence and insurance. Could I have those if I was here illegally?

Maybe he was illiterate, I say.

6.

I met Pierre at a Filipino church. I was new to Vancouver, trying to find a congregation with people my age who practised an informed Christianity. Including myself, there were three Black folks at the church that day. I remember Pierre's height, his fancy mixed-metal watch, his collared white shirt under a sweater. He was reserved when I spoke to him. The following week, I went back and he was there again. I asked him if he wanted to do something later, and I think we hiked a trail.

He said he'd been going to that church for five weeks and every week the members greeted him as if he were visiting for the first time. Every week, they asked him to stand and wave. At what point would he belong?

Over the next few years, Pierre and I spent every Saturday together, trying out churches in the region in the morning, making lunch, doing something outdoorsy in the afternoon, then watching a movie in the evening while eating heart attacks from Fatburger. We'd cycle through films by genre, through Kevin James, Kevin Hart, Denzel, Will,

Matt Damon. We had a horror-movie phase that ended with the truly terrible film *The Human Centipede*. He introduced me to Black French rap, waxed eulogistic about Kendrick and J. Cole on long drives out of the city.

We settled on a church in Richmond, not too far from the airport. That church has the greatest concentration of Black people either of us sees in a week, which is to say about ten.

7.

Only with clichés and the invincibility of youth can Pierre make sense of the disorienting incident with the officer.

He says, You never think this kind of stuff is going to happen to you. You know it *could* happen, just not to— He turns off the AC and opens the sunroof. So anyway, now I drive like this.

You didn't do anything wrong, I say.

I was speeding.

All right, yeah, fine.

I was trying to give him What He Needed. But it's hard to know with Pierre. His willingness to accept responsibility deflates me. It would be simpler to have this conversation if he were innocent and we could both make righteous fists against the police.

I go on, You realize that only 10 percent of that interaction had anything to do with speeding.

I know.

Even when you do something wrong, you're entitled to humane treatment, I say. Even Cain.

We both know the denouement of the Cain and Abel story. After God punishes him, Cain worries that someone will nevertheless kill him in retaliation. God says, No, if anyone kills you, I will take revenge. I promise. Here, I'm going to put a mark on you to warn folks not to harm you. Over time, the story gets perverted, and people—white people, no doubt—claim that Cain became the first Black man, meaning that Black people are cursed by God from the beginning, that we deserve everything we get, that our suffering is a kind of preordained, original karma. But in the original text, God actually intends the mark as a blessing, as a mitigation of Cain's suffering.

8.

Not to dwell too much on Cain, but when I teach Phillis Wheatley's poem "On Being Brought from Africa to America," I spend a long time on the closing couplet:

Remember, Christians, Negroes, black as Cain,
May be refined, and join the angelic train.

There's a lot to say: Wheatley appeals to the Christianity of her white audience. She sets herself at its mercy. Yet she also positions Christians and Negroes side by side so for a moment they're interchangeable; you're not sure which one is the subject. And, to the point, she plays into the misreading of Cain and Blackness, opting to have a bad soul rather than no soul at all. Even Cain deserves Christian treatment, she's arguing.

In America, I had a Hungarian church friend who loved the movie *Coming to America*. He learned English from it. My friend felt welcome in America. America laid out opportunities for him. He was able to start a business. He expanded. I always marvelled at how easily he was embraced as *American*, practically overnight, even with his accent, in a way that I or Pierre or any diasporic African would never be.

9.

I admit I was going fast, Pierre says again. But I was passing, so I thought I was going to get a warning. This guy gave me two tickets.

Two? I ask. For how much?

Pierre hesitates. He looks embarrassed. Finally, he says, For a thousand dollars.

A thousand!

To this day, I don't know what the second ticket is for.

10.

I tell Pierre about the times I have been stopped.

The first time was in Alabama. We had dropped off my brother at college for the fall semester. It was still dark, maybe 4:30 A.M., and we were at the beginning of a sixteen-hour drive back to Canada. A family friend was driving. My mother was in the passenger seat. I was in the back. A white officer pulled us over because we were driving below the speed limit on a road with no traffic. He asked us what we were doing there and where we were going. But he wouldn't let my mother speak. I'm not speaking to you, ma'am, he said, ostensibly because she wasn't driving. He didn't give us a ticket. We continued, feeling shaken and grateful. It's weird how we're so disoriented by these encounters that we leave them feeling grateful when, in fact, we should be furious, seeing as the officer had no basis on which he could give us a ticket.

During the last year of my doctorate, I was driving to a job at Humber College on the lakeshore of Toronto. A cop trailed me for a while. I was minutes from work. I thought, If I can just get to the parking lot of Humber, I'll be okay. Before I could get there, the cop pulled up beside me, and said, It's okay. You're clean. In an alternate memory of this incident, he stopped me and asked for my driver's licence and registration. He ran them through the system, before coming back and declaring, It's okay. You're clean. Maybe it happened twice? In any event, there was no reason for the random stop of me in my slightly rusted Civic. I taught my class, disoriented and stunned and inappropriately grateful, and hoped course evaluations would be kind.

Fifteen years later, in Vancouver, I got the only speeding ticket of my life, despite going the speed of traffic. The moment in Alabama is always with me, so I try not to be too fast or too slow. I wasn't looking at the speedometer, but I accepted the officer's assessment, which is not to say that I wasn't pitying myself, asking, Why me? Why me? while the other cars whizzed past us. I did dispute the ticket—the only time I've ever been to court. I got a sweet, paternal lecture from an Indian judge before he dismissed it.

I even told Pierre about my mother, whose car got hit from the back while she was exiting a gas station. Not long afterward, she ran into the back of someone else. In both cases, the police declared that she was in the wrong. Cumulatively, I have spent hours of uh-huh uh-huh conversation with her as she tried to understand, Why am I always in the wrong?

11.

There's more, Pierre says. The cop had my car towed.

Unnecessary, I say. Pierre doesn't drink or use any substances. He was only going twenty kilometres per hour above the speed limit, not racing along like some of the city's brightly coloured Lamborghinis and Ferraris. Or even Teslas.

I was left standing on the side of the road, Pierre says. The cop asked me if I had anyone to come get me. I said no.

You should've called me, I said.

You were busy. I didn't want to bother you.

I feel a rush of guilt. I am, sadly, one of those people who always claim to be busy or tired. About a month before the incident with the cop, Pierre had a flat tire and I missed his call because I was in the middle of a winding conversation with my mother. When I called him back, close to an hour later, I found out he was stranded on his way back from Whistler but had already arranged a tow truck. He was okay. Just a flat. He was probably remembering the last time he had a flat tire and we had figured out how to change it by watching YouTube videos in the parking garage of his college.

Still, I suspect it wasn't just busyness that deterred him from calling me. It was shame, already coursing its way through his self-perception.

Anyway, Pierre says. The cop called the tow truck and they towed my car and I had no choice—I had to get into the back of his car.

I imagine all six feet three inches of Pierre squished into the back seat, looking out the window, looking at his phone, looking anywhere but into the officer's reflected eyes.

I can't explain that feeling, he says. I felt like I was being arrested. My whole life, I never thought—

Encounters with the police feel like near-death experiences. You see the light. Your life flickers before your eyes like scenes of a montage. If something happened to you, who would know?

Pierre says, I saw my parents' faces.

12.

The cop dropped Pierre off at a gas station.

Pierre tells me that a man hit on him outside the gas station and he'd never been so happy to exchange one unwelcome advance for another.

He says, The gay guy asked me if I wanted a ride some-where.

You're sure he was gay? He wasn't just—

I *knew*. It was more than a *ride*. I knew what he was get-ting at, and I still almost got in his car.

This is the effect of his disorientation. He was about to risk entering another dangerous situation with a stranger just so he could get home to safety. Here was another role to play, this time in a gay, white, sexual fan-tasy: the exotic, hung Black man who could blow your back out.

13.

His vehicle was impounded for seven days. When he went to get it, Pierre expected the same hassle as with the police officer.

But it was easy, he says. I showed them proof, some ID, and two minutes later they let me have it.

He can't predict how the world works anymore. When will white bureaucracy step in to inconvenience him? When do minor infractions beget exaggerated consequences? When might he get lucky?

14.

I got home and for two weeks I couldn't do anything, Pierre explains.

That was the period he had described as his staycation.

I just watched Netflix, all the comedy specials I could find, trying to make myself happy again. I ate ice cream and sat in bed. I didn't work. Didn't call my family. Out of the blue, Pastor Ron called me. He was all friendly, didn't want anything. He said, Call me Ron.

On the morning of the day that Pierre tells me this story, the Zoom sermon was based on Micah 6:8: What does the Lord require of you, but to do justly, to love mercy, and to walk humbly with thy God? Pastor Ron said that justice meant holding yourself to the highest standard while extending mercy to those who fault you. In other words, police yourself, not other people.

It's very Martin Luther King.

15.

You know what I was listening to when the cop pulled me over?

Kendrick, I say. Pierre has been having a Kendrick Lamar renaissance.

Right, he says. So as this cop's coming toward the car, Kendrick's going—and at this point Pierre sings with his shoulders—We gonna be all *right*!

16.

Next time, I say, call me. It doesn't matter if I'm busy or

with someone or in an airport somewhere. Just call me if anything happens.

He is quiet.

I feel the futility of trying to protect a Black person from danger. *If anything happens.* If Pierre had been shot or Tasered in his car, what could I do? It is already too late. Maybe I'm insistent because I don't want to learn of his death on the news. I want this young Black man to be distinguishable from other endangered young Black men. He is so soft-spoken that you constantly have to ask him to repeat himself. He quit his job after three months and started his own business when he realized he could do everything the firm was doing on his own. He likes his pants cut just above the ankle. Never wears socks. Can identify the model and sometimes the year of every car on the road at a glance. Became boyish when I bought him a toy car for his last birthday. The cop's version of resisting arrest would be the only one in circulation.

I say, Next time—

It's so sad to have to say *next time*.

I try again: Next time, the minute you're pulled over, start recording on your phone. When the cop gets to the window, let him know that you are recording this interaction. He knows the time we're living in. He knows if he doesn't act correct—if he doesn't treat you like everyone else—he's gonna be all over the Internet, that the repercussions are finally real.

I've taken on the tone of the righteously indignant.

But, again, I've missed the target.

Pierre says, I looked him up when I got home. He's

been fired twice. He was involved in some kind of corruption thing.

And he's back on the streets. Tell me, how does that happen?

Yeah, I don't know.

17.

I'm the third person whom Pierre has told about the incident.

He told two specific African friends: one studying in the Philippines and another who studied in Maine before going back to Africa. Why them? Why me? I think it's for the same reason Black people acknowledge each other in the street or create a Black club in high school. We need each other to anchor ourselves against waves of racial disorientation. It sometimes baffles white people, this intimacy between Black people, even strangers. We seem to be affirming each other *only* because we are Black when, in fact, we are affirming to the other that I see you as *more* than Black.

Have you told your parents? I ask.

No way, he says. Not even my brother.

I can understand why. His parents would tell him to forget about North America, just come back to Africa, for his safety and his dignity.

My mother tries to get my brother back to Canada at every opportunity, not really for her sake—he doesn't have to live near her—but just to increase his chances of staying alive. So far, he's outlived her fears in Alabama and North Carolina. He works out and eats well and hopefully will die of natural causes. That's as optimistic as I can be about his future in America.

18.

We make it back to Vancouver.

In the elevator of my building, he sniffs upward. I smell it too.

Someone's been to Church's Chicken, he says. Not KFC. Church's.

I laugh. So specific. We're aware of what Americans think about Black people and fried chicken, a stereotype that neither of us knew until moving to the continent. But we also think the Church's Chicken on Fraser Street is brilliantly designed: glass everywhere so you can practically read the menu from the street, private drive-through, bright-yellow sign floating like Christ the Redeemer over Rio.

In my condo, neither of us eats. We watch a comedy special where a white woman is funny until she says, I'm from the South, but I'm not a Southern belle, not until I need to be. Then we watch a Black man who says, I'm split: I can't be a Democrat because I'm a Christian and I can't be a Republican because I'm Black.

And so we shut off YouTube and Pierre tells me another driving story.

When I went back to my country for my sister's wedding, he says, I was driving somewhere to pick up some gifts. It was midnight, no one was on the road, and I was speeding. There was a cop parked off the road in a spot where he could see me but I couldn't see him. And he caught me. He came up to me and said, Good night. I said, Good night. He told me that I was speeding. I didn't deny it. It was true. But I did tell him about the wedding and the gifts and that I could see ahead of me for hundreds of metres. The cop looked at me and he could tell that I wasn't drunk. And you know what? He didn't give me a ticket. He said, I'm gonna let you go. But don't speed again, all right? Like a dad. And you know what? I didn't speed. I saw him parked in the same spot on my way back and I waved at him and he waved back.

It's almost midnight when Pierre decides to leave my place and drive home.

He does not message to let me know whether he arrives safely.

And a Mouth

The French horn

At the end of grade six, the kids who signed up for band gathered in the school gym to select our instruments. The girls asked for flute or clarinet. The boys asked for saxophone or drums. The instrument I really wanted was violin, but this was band, not orchestra.

One by one, the music teacher called us to the front and ran us through a little audition that involved matching the pitch that she sang. The pitch test was to determine which students had the best ears to play brass instruments. After the test, she announced which instrument each student was assigned.

When the music teacher got to *W*, I went up and tried to match the note she sang.

Mmm, she hummed.

Muhh, I hummed back.

Mee, she hummed.

Meh, I tried to match.

Weird, she said. You're singing everything a third below me. What do you want to play?

Saxophone, I said.

Everybody can't play the saxophone and flute, she said. We need people to play trombone and baritone.

I thought a while, then I said, Can I play French horn?

It was one of the least popular instruments. I only asked because I had a crush on a girl who was assigned to French horn.

The music teacher shook her head. I supposed I had failed the pitch test. I was prepared to try again.

She said, The mouthpiece is too small for you. Then, with a stutter of mind, she added, But you've got this great deep mouth. I wish we could get you a bassoon.

I didn't know what that was. It sounded too close to baboon. The teacher wrote something on her clipboard.

Tenor sax, she said for me.

I walked back to my spot in the crowd of students, disoriented. Were my lips really too big to play the French horn?

The tenor saxes sat in the back row of band with the trombones, the baritones, and the bass clarinets. The French horns sat in the row ahead, in the corner of my left eye. I could comfortably see the girl I liked, one hand tucked into the bell of the horn, happily puffing her French horn or emptying the slides of spit. It was a fine piece of machinery, the horn. Yet it sounded like a lonely animal in a foggy forest.

I went to the public library and read up on the instrument. I borrowed cassettes of classical music. I made myself a tiny mouthpiece out of a Christmas ornament, a bell, to practise my embouchure. I was prepared to work twice as hard to get half as far, to quote Blackparentese.

The following year, I asked for the French horn again.

This time, the music teacher said fine.

And I was terrible. In my mouth, the instrument gurgled and bubbled with spit. It demanded a lot of pressure from my diaphragm. It made my teeth vibrate, my whole face buzz. There was no medieval forest in the instrument, only a series of wet diarrhea farts. I got a C in music that semester. And that wasn't happening, girl or no girl, so I switched back to tenor sax and all was right with the world.

Except for the question of my lips.

Of course, I understand now that I was a poor French horn player because of my ears, not my lips. I simply couldn't hear and match the notes I was supposed to play. Forget leaping from one note to another if they had the same fingering. Of course, I know that dazzling Black brass players exist. My uncle and my cousin both play trumpet. And despite those facts, the music teacher's assessment weighs on me. She seemed to prophesy from the beginning that I was not anatomically suitable for the instrument. Maybe I was naive to think that my lips could purse or vibrate like all those thin-lipped white kids. I wish that I had proven her wrong and overcome systemic biases through determination. But this is a story of defeat.

Biological determinism, the belief that our abilities and behaviour are fixed by our genes, and racism go hand in hand. Linking physical characteristics to musical potential is an example of how race gets tangled up with everyday pursuits. After that assessment, I believed that I had physical limits and physical advantages linked to my race, sometimes simultaneously. When I sank in pools, people said, You're so lucky, you don't have a shred of fat on you. Biological determinism dictated that I couldn't swim but that I could sprint. As proof, it offered that the three fastest sprinters in my grade were all Black. The Fastest Kid was phenomenal at all sports, in fact, first pick and team captain always, and we all knew that he was robbed (see Taylor Swift/Beyoncé, MTV Awards *circa* 2009) when he didn't win Best Athlete at the end of middle school. The prize instead went to a white kid who was aiiight—skilled, agreeable, smart, attractive, a textbook all-rounder. I saw the Fastest Kid outside a walk-in clinic twenty-five years later. He was a star athlete through high school, but hadn't gone pro or anything. As we talked, it became clear that the major force that determined his life was not biological at all, but economic.

Braces

Around the time of the French horn fiasco, there was a civil war in my mouth. Northern teeth against southern teeth. Big teeth versus tiny jaw. A widening ideological gap between my front teeth. Multiple teeth settling the same land. Overcrowding that led to unsanitary conditions.

My mother insisted that we get my teeth fixed.

You can't go through life with teeth like that, she said. She loved us, and although all identities intersect with beauty, my mother knew that living as a Black person in

North America meant being judged immediately by what's on your surface.

I wore braces for about six years, two years longer than I needed to, in my estimation. After four, my teeth were straight and it was clear that braces were not going to solve the bite problem. The delay at the orthodontist was not about teeth, but about money. My teeth would stay incarcerated until my family had paid the uttermost farthing.

In those days, each patient received a paper chart where the orthodontist would record the treatment. At a glance, he could look over his instructions and my progress. Once insurance ran out, the staff stapled past-due notices to the front of my chart. Each visit, they ripped off the old notice and stapled an updated notice with a record of their attempts to get payment. My chart was covered in staples. Countless raised scars. I tried to hold my chart in such a way that the other patients wouldn't see, or put it face down on the tray so the attending dentist wouldn't notice the record of poverty. But the chief orthodontist, when he made his rounds, would always read the history of finances before looking at me. What's going on there? he'd ask me. I'd mumble or shrug, embarrassed in front of the white children. Then he'd read the history of treatment, look into my mouth for a few seconds, and write, *Adj.* Adjust.

I wish the history of my mouth was simply of eating and smiling and talking and laughing, and not a site of biological determinism or, in this case, economics. My mouth represents a past of poverty, of monthly pain as regular as rent. It represents my parents' investment in future prosperity. Good teeth meant I could stand a chance at an interview and secure a job, buy a place to live, and onward into the echelons of the middle class. Through my mouth, the pre-requisites and unpleasant reality of Black–white relations were translated. Never was there the thought that I might be the one interviewing another or determining the class of another person. I needed straight teeth because I would need to smile at someone who held my future in their hands.

Smile

I almost always smile in photos. When I don't smile in photos, people say I look angry or sad or tired. I've also heard *scary*. The same thing happens to the speaker in Claudia Rankine's *Citizen*. A friend sees a photograph and "wants to know why you look so angry." The speaker thinks she looks relaxed. But the friend is made uncom-fortable by an unsmiling Black person "and he needs you to account for that."

I've accounted by almost always smiling. At some point, post-braces, I stood in front of a mirror and practised all the smiles available to me and chose teeth, very wide, slight eye squint. The last detail came from Tyra, who taught the world to *smize*, to smile with their eyes.

There are many reasons why I smile, but few involve happiness. I hereby notify you that I will not rob your store. I will not come after you in this parking garage. I will not stay too long or take up too much space in this coffee shop. I'm not carrying anything that can be used as a weapon. I will not assault you in this elevator. Aren't my teeth lovely? I will not bite you with my expensive teeth. As you can see, most reasons involve not being a threat.

But I would like to have the privilege of a neutral face.

For all of my efforts to smile, I've developed a frown. People mirror back the frown more readily than they mirror the smile, although the frown is far less complicated: I have slight astigmatism that I don't correct with my contact prescription, so I frown a little to sharpen people into focus. What concerns me is that these expressions, smiling or frowning, are not in fact expressive. I don't do these things because I am happy or angry. As a Black man, expression as a sign of my feelings is secondary to the reception of my face. When I smile, my face is the performance of a face conditioned to be agreeable in order to advance. In other places, parts of America, for example, the performance of facial mugging or facial docility would be a matter of survival. To be honest, when the pandemic hit, I didn't fuss that we all had to wear masks. My mouth was one less thing to worry about. Wasn't I wearing a mask anyway?

A NOSE

When Michael Jackson died, a rumour resurfaced that he had no nose, that it had collapsed years ago and he had been wearing a prosthetic nose over a hole in his face.

My whole life I've suffered from problematic breathing.

I wake up in the morning full of phlegm. As a child, I used to get head colds while my brother got chest colds. I don't have asthma. I don't have allergies. I breathe through my mouth when my mind drifts. Until recently, I was excluded from luxury diagnoses like sleep apnea. Doctors don't take your symptoms seriously if your body is Black. One dentist advised me, Just try harder to breathe through your nose.

Try harder.

So when, under police restraint, New York cigarette seller Eric Garner and Minneapolis cigarette buyer George Floyd wheezed, I can't breathe, I can't breathe, I had a physical reaction. Not only did I recognize the Blackness of their bodies, the hazard of their gender, I felt the sensations of those final moments—wanting air but being obstructed, wanting the stabilizing yawn of a deep breath, wanting to breathe as easily as the people around you.

In their slow deaths, the men were unable to help themselves—they could not try harder to live—and they received no help from others.

George Floyd's death took eight minutes and forty-six seconds. Because America is still America, you can now buy T-shirts with this number.

Like many anaesthetics, propofol works so quickly that in ten seconds you can be unconscious.

Michael Jackson's doctor claims that he administered the drug after Jackson begged for it, monitored him for ten minutes, went to the bathroom, and two minutes later, when he returned, Jackson was dead.

To be precise, people don't die of an overdose, of

propofol toxicity, not exactly. They die because propofol induces "respiratory depression." Another source calls it "airway obstruction."

In response to an Instagram post about the disparate treatment of George Floyd in Minneapolis and white supremacist and mass murderer Dylann Roof in Charleston, someone with a private account comments, "George Floyd died from a drug overdose, read the autopsy report."

Could one believe a man is suffocating and continue to asphyxiate him unless one wanted to kill him?

I wonder—in my need to make sense of the senseless—whether the police officers thought Floyd and Garner were faking their distress. Did they think this was a performance? Do they find our reality unconvincing and implausible? To white people, does Black agony seem exaggerated? Staged?

* * *

At his Super Bowl halftime performance in 1993, Jackson leaped out on the stage and stood still for two minutes. Imagine the temerity of such a move at a live show, a sporting event no less—standing still for that long. His stillness became a statement.

When he finally moved, it was a simple turn of the head, to give us another angle, as if he was saying, *Go ahead, take a good look at me. Take me in.*

Ten days later, in her famous 1993 interview with Jackson, Oprah asks about the change to the colour of his skin. Jackson says he has a skin disorder that destroys the pigment in his skin (later confirmed by his autopsy). Then he adds, "What about all the millions of people who sit out in the sun to become darker, to become other than what they are? Nobody says nothing about that."

About his nose, he becomes equally defensive.

Oprah says, "You had your nose done, obviously."

Jackson, sharply: "Yeah, but so did a lot of people that I know."

His irritation in both cases seems rooted in the double standard whereby white celebrities have cosmetic procedures without too big a fuss while he, a Black celebrity, becomes tabloid fodder. To be sure, he's neglecting the scale of his fame and the nature of his surgery, but he does make a point. Nose surgery on a Black person signifies way more in the popular imagination than a facelift does. I hardly need to state the assumption: he's trying to be white.

This assumption continues to circulate, although the most common facial cosmetic surgery procedure is rhinoplasty for white and Black people alike. It persists even when the language of ethnic surgeries softens from *whiteness* to *Westernization*. It persists although doctors report that Black clients "desire some form of nasal refinement without loss of their ethnic identity." Black patients ask for reduced width, nasal tip definition, and higher projection. They don't want to look like Michael, Janet, or Latoya Jackson with the pinched nose of the 1980s.

Playing out on our noses are major questions: What is universal? What is individual? What is the relationship between the two?

More broadly, the nose, the mouth, and the eyes are common, universal features of humans that we point to as evidence of our equality. It's a rather rhetorically elegant, if oversimplified, response to the pseudo-science that ascribes significance to phenotypical differences among humans. It's so obvious, it's clichéd. Aren't I human? Look, I have two eyes, a nose, and a mouth. The other comparable cliché is: If you cut me, won't I bleed?

Despite the equal distribution of eyes, noses, and mouths among individuals, their variations have nevertheless been used to foment division and classification. We may all have noses, but your nose is not like mine. When the white nose is held up as the standard nose, as the default nose, as the Platonic golden nose, then any variation becomes deviation—which is a hop from *deviant*, a skip from *devious*, and a jump to *demonic*, until simple variety becomes a stairway to hell.

* * *

The nose, the skin, and the hair are major sites of racial migration. Michael Jackson is not the only Black celebrity to transform himself through those features.

In 2016, Lil' Kim posted photos to her Instagram that left fans shocked. Her hair was blond, her skin was bleached, her nose was slimmed. She assumed the coy angles and postures of white Instagram models and further processed herself through filters. It was the end of the Obama years and people had been throwing around *postracial*. Is this what postracial looked like? Rachel Dolezal had been exposed the year before. Was there a new category of *transracial* emerging?

Treasure, a Black teenager, believes she is white. Her mother brings her on *Dr. Phil* for help.

In the pre-recorded segments, we learn that Treasure is not simply under the impression that she is white; she is, in fact, a white supremacist.

She says, "When it comes to Black people, I think they're all ugly and I have nothing in common with them." And: "My nose is not giant like African-Americans'." Her mother informs us that Treasure used to decapitate her Black dolls or make them the slaves of her white dolls.

The audience is stunned. How to explain this? Quite likely, Treasure has ingested serious anti-Black propaganda. Possibly, she has a mental disorder (such as borderline or narcissistic personality disorder or sociopathic tendencies) that is expressed most visibly on this issue. Maybe this behaviour is a manifestation of grief over the death of her white stepfather. Possibly, it's a hoax. That's what her sister claims.

Nevertheless, Treasure is asking the same question that Michael Jackson and Lil' Kim pose with their bodies. Can we migrate from one race to another? It's important to note that the direction of these transracial desires is overwhelmingly from Black to white. When a white person expresses something similar, they may be accused of "acting" Black rather than trying to be Black. When a Black person "acts" white, it's assumed that they want to *be* white. The movement to whiteness seems to be aspirational, while the movement to Blackness is only provisional, temporary, to be put on and taken off when Blackness becomes inconvenient.

I can't definitively explain why some people of colour wish to be white. The reasons vary. Treasure's reasons will differ from Michael Jackson's or Lil' Kim's. Moreover, the desire is so coated in disapproval that it can never be expressed. Yet I imagine that a cluster of reasons involves ease: to have opportunities appear, to move through life more easily, to be treated better (or just fairly) at first sight, and to have the barrier of their appearance disappear.

There's a difference between wanting to be white and wanting to be human. The error of transracial desires like Treasure's lies in the assumption that being white is the same as being a human. People of colour don't want to be white; we want to exist at full value—and the only people who seem to occupy that class of existence are white folks, hence the metonymic slip.

Treasure's YouTube name is Treasure the White Queen.

* * *

The King of Pop. Most of us have never seen Michael Jackson in flesh and blood or in a context outside performance or tabloid. From our vantage, beholding celebrity, he's all persona.

The word *persona* comes to us from the Latin word for mask. *Person*, *personality*, *personal*, though ostensibly marking authenticity, all emerge from the same make-believe place.

It's possible to characterize Jackson's physical changes as a kind of fusion of persona and person, of art and artist, under the hegemony of whiteness. Yet he seemed to be reaching beyond whiteness; his ambitions seemed not transracial but transhuman, more metaphysical than physical, more futuristic in his theatrical military getups than present.

Two Eyes

Portrait

I mentioned that I attended an arts high school. My particular field was visual art. The curriculum included an art history component that began with the cave paintings of Lascaux and ended in the present. By grade twelve, we had worked our way up to modernism. We drew the blinds and sat in the dark to look at slides. Picasso and Braque and Gris and Miró burst upon us. Suddenly, there was African art—but no African artist. Everything African was filtered through white men. The word appropriation never came up. The presence of Blackness in European art was cast as revolutionary, rebellious, radical. Blackness didn't share the same language as, say, the gentle Japanese influence on Impressionist art. And looking at the faces of Les Demoiselles d'Avignon, at the discoloured, distorted, inexpressive faces, I understood, through no fault of my teacher, that the African presence is what made modern art ugly, upsetting to most viewers. It's what caused art to fall apart.

Some years later, the Sudanese model Alek Wek interrupted the modelling world with her dark skin, round face, short hair, with her small eyes, flat nose, large lips. The fashion industry congratulated itself on smashing beauty standards. But André Leon Talley, editor of American *Vogue* at the time and a Black man, was not duped: "It's a unique kind of beauty that the world is not ready for that. [*sic*] The world is saying it's multicultural and global but it's not ready for that look, I don't think, on a broad scale." On Wek's youthful optimism about being embraced by the modelling world, he said, "She's naive. She's having a naive vision because there are obviously prejudices against her look." He believed she was being used as proof of diversity. One Black face was not enough to undo centuries of white aesthetic bias. In fact, Wek's "unique kind of beauty" points to something more sinister at work. Her presence as the representative of Blackness among the sheer number of conventionally beautiful white faces was inscribing the racial idea of the superiority of white beauty. Ask anyone who they'd prefer to look like, Alek Wek or any other model on that runway. I say the following only because I feel protective of Wek. I think we are being mocked by a white fashion industry that uses her face like a substitute for blackface.

In high school, the only way I could get to Blackness and beauty was through whiteness. Our art class took a big-deal, cross-border field trip to the Albright–Knox Art Gallery in Buffalo. There I stood before a painting, *The Servant Girl*, by my favourite artist in my teens and twenties, Amedeo

Modigliani, who himself owed a lot to African art. The servant girl is a white girl in a black dress who stands with her hands clasped in front of her. Her face and neck are elongated in typical Modigliani style. The only warm colour comes from her face, her hands, and her eyes. Her eyes are blued out—the entire eyeball, not just the iris, is painted blue. If you asked me why that painting resonates with me so much, back then I would have answered somewhat narcissistically: the elongation of the servant's face resembles mine; the colour of her skin looks tropical; I recognize that posture of servitude. But now, I am moved primarily by those eyes, the naive and sickly blindness of them. I am looking at a girl whose eyes have yielded to the beauty of colour rather than the usefulness of purpose. She can't look outward from them. She can't even see herself.

In studio, I patterned my work on Modigliani's. For my final self-portrait (every year we had to produce one), I drew myself embracing myself. Both Ians look alien and androgynous. My skin is orange. The entire portrait is stippled with pastel, a technique borrowed from the Impressionists. I used no black; instead, I mixed colours with their complementary colours to give the illusion of black, another technique borrowed from the Impressionists. Up close, the stippling makes me look as if I were made of rain. Took forever. And in the portrait, my eyes, all four of them, are shades of blue. Odd. I had seen Toni Morrison's book *The Bluest Eye* on a storage cart in English class. The title stuck with me, as did the cover of the Plume edition, with Pecola sitting hunched in a red sweater. The book wasn't assigned to my class and I didn't read it until years later, so I didn't know anything beyond the jacket copy. Nevertheless, I gave myself the bluest eyes out of a kind of fascination with Modigliani's blighted portraits and solidarity with Pecola and Morrison, whose novel was the *only* Black book that crossed my path— and accidentally at that—in high school.

As I was working on the eyes of the self-portrait, classmates came by and asked, Why are your eyes blue? I said something about contrast with orange, something about transparency.

There were many important questions beneath that question. Do you know what you look like? You know your eyes can't and won't ever be blue, right? And the biggie: Are you self-loathing?

Self-loathing, no. I can't say I wanted to be white. I was lonely and insecure socially, sure. I was the only Black kid in my class, throughout high school, so I drew two of me, for company. And I was acknowledging in that self-portrait that there was something wrong with my vision, much like the blindness—or the inward gaze?—of Modigliani's *The Servant Girl*. I couldn't tell you what exactly at the time, but it was akin to seeing too much of one colour, then closing one's eyes and seeing its opposite. Something in me was resisting the normalization of being the only Black person in a sea of white people.

My art career ended after high school. The self-portrait is hanging in a bathroom in my mother's house, over the toilet, next to the mirror. I see it whenever I step out of the shower.

How do you get blue eyes? For a child to have blue eyes requires that both parents carry the recessive gene, meaning that there's likely someone white on each side of the family. When Black people have children with blue eyes—you can do the historical math.

But there's another way. Tameka Harris, a.k.a. Tiny, a singer better known for her reality show with her husband, the rapper T.I., had surgery to make her eyes blue. She says they're ice grey. Fine. To change her eyes, she flew to Africa, where a doctor slit her eyes and inserted a coloured implant.

The procedure is not legal in North America, though I suspect not simply for medical reasons.

Uncle Larry

My white uncle by marriage made a joke. It was his first trip to Trinidad, part of a tour to charm our family, and by all reviews he was succeeding. Such a nice English man. Affable. Very friendly. Not like most white people. Also: muscular. His joke:

What do you call a Rasta who prescribes glasses and a Rasta who wears glasses?

A Rasta for eyes and a Rasta *four* eyes.

Sorry. It was the eighties. Jokes weren't as funny then.

Neither my brother nor I got it. Nobody in the family wore glasses or knew the expression *four eyes*. We were stuck on the Rasta part. What did being a Rasta have to do with anything? He was trying to make the joke relevant to us. But perhaps he didn't realize that Rastas were more Jamaican than Trinidadian and, even so, the Trini Rastafarians belonged to another class of society, which as children we were warned about. The joke fell flat because he was eliding Black people, Jamaicans and Trinidadians, eliding various classes. Could he not see differences?

Uncle Larry's eyes were very blue and his skin was very red and he had packed exercise springs and a resistant grip strengthener to work his chest and forearms. My aunt seemed happy with him but not in awe. I couldn't imagine having to look into his blue eyes every day or hold his red, hairy hand or kiss him. And that was as much as I knew married people did. Intimacy seemed impossible.

Why was he so comfortable? Why did he brush away formality so quickly? We expected a more uptight British man. His personality was incongruous with our expectations of his brand of whiteness. We expected this kind of joking from Americans, like the white boy in my class whose nose was always running and who licked up his snot. The Trinidadian kids carried embroidered handkerchiefs.

The white boy

In Trinidad, we had two white students in our school, a girl and her younger brother who were in the same grade as my brother and me. They had blue eyes. The snot-eating boy, Jeremy, was best friends with the guy I wanted to be best friends with, and this conferred on him a kind of rarefied status. In the socio-economics of childhood, I had status too, as one of the smart kids (kids weren't bullied in Trini culture for that), but I was younger than both of them, having skipped grade three, and therefore risky best-friend material.

Jeremy bore the unreasonable responsibility of embodying all the bits of information I had picked up about white people, and his behaviour, in turn, was taken as representative of all white people. He had an accent, like all white people. I found his eye contact excessive. Every sentence, every conversation, every day.

His physical presence attuned me, even at that age, to my expectations of whiteness. I expected him to be the smartest, the cleanest, but not the kindest. He had an aura, not of his own making, but of ours. Colonized people who live at a distance from white people nevertheless have strong myths that govern our expectations of and interactions with them. The myth, which they themselves are responsible for, says that they are all intelligent, but we discover that they are only articulate. And the more we listen, the more we realize that they are not articulate, but confident, self-advocating, garrulous, and accented.

Niece, nephew

When people look at my biracial niece and nephew, they will find themselves smiling involuntarily.

My niece has curly dark-brown hair and large brown Disney eyes. She will be enviably thin in her teen years. Her skin is what white folks call olive or Mediterranean. Black folks call it light. My nephew also has curly hair, down to his chin, but blond. His eyes are blue. He's about the same complexion as his sister.

When the kids are alone with my brother, their race gets

interpreted through him. The term is *cladisticizing*: "racially perceiving someone by inquiring into their family history." My brother tells me about going to restaurants and having people approach to say, What beautiful children you have! What they really mean, what makes the children beautiful, are those white elements—the blond hair, the pale skin, the blue eyes—Photoshopped onto their otherwise Black bodies. It has not been my experience that people are going up to Black kids or their parents to tell them they're beautiful.

My niece and nephew will occasionally be misapprehended as white. Neither of them is trying to pass. There is no deception on their part. People will project whatever they want to see onto their bodies. Their shares in whiteness will give them advantages that non-biracial Black kids will not have. In those little graces within a conversation, those areas where physical presence sways the outcome, they will fare better than Black kids. And between the two of them, forgive me for this indelicacy, my nephew, being male and blue-eyed and fair-haired, will find an even more receptive world.

Or, who knows, the world could be radically different and this prophecy will prove anachronistic. I'll try to explain the surface-level judgments of the past to my nephew and he'll say, Oh no, Uncle, that's impossible. That must have been all in your head.

Life Certificate

My mother needs to prove that she is alive.

I don't understand why you have to do this, I say.

For my benefit, she says.

It's not for your benefit.

For my pension.

She tells me that the pension office requires a life certificate to protect itself against fraud from identity theft. There are people who profit from impersonating dead people. I try to imagine what kind of person could convincingly pretend to be my mother.

The life certificate form requires a witness.

I'd ask you to be my witness, she says. But you're not free.

So she drives to a friend's house. He signs the form. She scans it and e-mails it to the pension office and forgets about it. Her life returns to its cycle of supplements and twenty-four-hour news stations.

A few days later, she receives a response. Her life certificate has been rejected.

I say, A form can't be the only way to prove you're alive.

Look, she says, the form is not the problem. I just need to get it notarized.

* * *

Later that week, my mother messages me. She found a judge.

I send a thumbs-up emoji.

She messages, He's a Justice of the Peace.

I send another thumb. I don't know the difference between *Judge* and *Justice*. I message, Is this man qualified to tell you whether you're alive?

She doesn't reply. A few minutes pass.

Are you there? I ask.

She does not reappear.

To prove her identity, she takes government photo ID to the Justice, even though she doesn't think the photo on her licence captures her likeness. The resemblance is good enough for him. He notarizes the form. My mother scans it, e-mails it, forgets about it. She takes her calcium. She watches shootings.

The pension office responds. Rejected.

It's like a Kafka story, I say.

They don't accept scans, she says.

I groan into the phone. What if you went to the pension office in person?

They need the original, notarized form.

You are the original, though.

This time, the mailed, notarized, original form causes a pension to trickle into her account. But the funds stop after six months. She needs a new life certificate, the pension office informs her.

Every six months, my mother needs to prove that she is alive. She would go back to the Justice who previously notarized her to prove it. But he has died. Now she has to find someone else.

More Than Half of Americans Can't Swim

"I have come to believe." Audre Lorde, "The Transformation of Silence into Language and Action," *Sister Outsider: Essays and Speeches* (New York: Crossing Press, 2007), 40.

at least two million Black people died. Estimates vary. This one is from digitalhistory.uh.edu/disp_textbook.cfm?smtID=2&psid=3034.

Instagram post that a friend forwarded to me. Here's some more context from the original poster, trying to explain what they intended:

"ghostdumps: Hello. A lot is going on, and I felt the need to say something. Again I wish to reiterate, people aren't obligated to post on their social media what they're doing to help the cause—but i know a lot of people who hide behind their excuses because they are uncomfortable. You're not a bad person for not sharing these things but now more than ever, if you are in a place of privilege, please reconsider using your voice and platform, however small it may be, to help. Spread donation and petition links. Educate. Have these uncomfortable conversations with the people around you. Teach yourself to erase the racism that is built deep inside of you, inside of everyone. Do not be ashamed. Black people are dying. And their lives matter. #BLM #justiceforgeorgefloyd I have tagged some great people on Instagram that have done a really good job at educating and showing us what's going on. There's no excuse! LAST SLIDE IS A QUOTE FROM ANGELA DAVIS HERSELF. READ ABOUT HER.

EDUCATE YOURSELF. She has an insane amount of helpful books that will completely change your outlook on this situation rn. (EDIT: link in my bio with a full list of resources to educate yourself on how to be a white or nonblack ally, and how to actively be non racist, among other helpful readings) // Title page illustrated by the lovely Emmy Hamilton of @cowpetter and @m0mzines."
The full post can be found at instagram.com/p/CA0zhFzFjLf.

Consider David Foster Wallace. All quotations in this section are from "Authority and American Usage," *Consider the Lobster and Other Essays* (New York: Back Bay Books, 2005), 108–9.

"The master's tools." Audre Lorde, "The Master's Tools Will Never Dismantle the Master's House," *Sister Outsider: Essays and Speeches* (New York: Crossing Press, 2007), 112.

"Survival is not an academic skill" and *"Difference must not be merely tolerated."* Ibid., 112, 111.

"little, fat, black man." Marcus Garvey is quoting Du Bois's insult in "W.E.B. Du Bois as a Hater of Dark People" (1923), in *Call and Response: Key Debates in African American Studies*, eds. Henry Louis Gates, Jr., and Jennifer Burton (New York: W.W. Norton, 2011), 262.

"It is no wonder." Ibid., 263.

"the most dangerous enemy of the Negro race." W.E.B. Du Bois, "Marcus Garvey: A Lunatic or a Traitor?" (1924), in *Call and Response*, 266.

"War, horrible as it is, might be preferable." Martin Luther King, Jr. "My Pilgrimage to Nonviolence" (1958), in *Call and Response*, 560.

"nonviolence offers the only road to freedom."
Here's a fuller statement of King's reasoning for non-violence:
"Anyone leading a violent conflict must be willing to make a similar assessment [as the Vietnam War] regarding the

possible casualties to a minority population confronting a well armed, wealthy majority with a fanatical right wing that is capable of exterminating the entire black population and which would not hesitate such an attempt if the survival of white Western materialism were at stake."
Martin Luther King, Jr. "Nonviolence: The Only Road to Freedom" (1966), in *Call and Response*, 579.

"Like most people, I had heard of Gandhi" and *"half-dozen books on Gandhi's life and works."* King, "My Pilgrimage to Nonviolence," 561.

Disorientation

"So you're waiting." The quotation continues: "The first time you glimpse yourself through the eyes of a person like that, it's a cold moment." Kazuo Ishiguro, *Never Let Me Go* (Toronto: Vintage, 2010), 36.

"violent blow on the head." Venture Smith, *A Narrative of the Life and Adventures of Venture, a Native of Africa, but Resident above Sixty Years in the United States of America, Related by Himself* (1798), Project Gutenberg, gutenberg.org/1/0/0/7/10075.

"motionless on the deck." Olaudah Equiano, *The Interesting Narrative of the Life of Olaudah Equiano, or Gustavus Vassa, the African Written by Himself* (1789), Project Gutenberg, gutenberg.org/1/5/3/9/15399.

"Then it dawned upon me with a certain suddenness." W.E.B. Du Bois, *The Souls of Black Folk* (1903), Project Gutenberg, gutenberg.org/4/0/408.

"the flag to which you have pledged allegiance." "James Baldwin vs. William F. Buckley: A Legendary Debate from 1965," YouTube video posted August 13, 2019, youtube.com/watch?v=5Tek9h3a5wQ.

"I felt, but did not yet understand." Ta-Nehisi Coates, *Between the World and Me* (New York: Spiegel & Grau, 2015), 21.

"I needed some time to think." Ibram X. Kendi, *How to Be an Antiracist* (New York: One World, 2019), 45, 47. To Kendi's disorienting experience, I would add that injustice or unfairness is not, in fact, arbitrary. The concept of fairness assumes a system that is predictable and transparent. The issue is that we've been linking punishment to *why* rather than *who*. If instead of asking *why* Ted is being punished, one notes *who* is being punished, one will discover that *who* gets punished is extremely predictable even though the *why* might be arbitrary. Racial discrimination is both predictable (Black folks will be treated worse) and unpredictable (but not all the time, not explicitly, because we're not supposed to be treated unfairly).

"maybe being black could suck a little bit." Quoted in Baratunde Thurston, *How to Be Black* (New York: HarperCollins, 2012), 29.

"far too shocked to have any real reaction." James Baldwin, *Notes of a Native Son* (Boston: Beacon Press, 2012), 165.

"The disaffection, the demoralization." "James Baldwin vs. William Buckley."

anti-Black racism as the weather. Sharpe extends the metaphor:
    "In what I am calling the weather, anti-Blackness is
    pervasive as climate. The weather necessitates changeability
    and improvisation; it is the atmospheric condition of time
    and place; it produces new ecologies."
See chapter 4 of *In the Wake: On Being and Blackness* (Durham, NC: Duke University Press, 2016) or read an excerpt at The New Inquiry (website), thenewinquiry.com/the-weather.

I just didn't see you. This scenario is paraphrased from Claudia Rankine's *Citizen* (Minneapolis, MN: Graywolf Press, 2014), 77.

Why go and make the incident out to be a microaggression? The term *microaggression* is fairly popular now, but as background:

the term was invented in 1970 by Chester Pierce and popularized by Claudia Rankine to describe the numerous hostilities enacted against Black people. Ibram X. Kendi prefers to call *microaggressions* outright *racist abuse.* A related term for the perplexing position of Asian Americanness is *minor feelings* (that term's from Cathy Park Hong).

Yet there's nothing micro or minor about the effect of race in these grey interactions. We can spend days getting our heads back on right.

Ten Bullets on Whiteness

"One can never really see into the heart." James Baldwin, "The Black Boy Looks at the White Boy," *Collected Essays*, ed. Toni Morrison (New York: Library of America, 1998), 284.

Whiteness also exists as a cluster of ethnicities. Hamid Dabashi writes an accessible, though very opinionated, article on the subject.

   If anything, it's worth checking out his additional sources:

   In his monumental two-volume study, *The Invention of the White Race* (revised edition, 2012), as early as in the 1960s Theodore W. Allen had documented the manner in which the ruling elite in the United States had devised the category of "white people" by way of economic exploitation of the African slaves and the social control of the emerging polities. More recently, in her *Birth of a White Nation: The Invention of White People and Its Relevance Today* (2013), Jacqueline Battalora has offered an examination of the enduring issue of race in the US tracing it back to when "white people" were invented through legislations and enactment of laws.

Hamid Dabashi, "The Invention of the White People," AlJazeera.com, August 28, 2017, aljazeera.com/indepth/opinion/2017/08/invention-white-people-170824095046840.html.

The people are disposable. The poor, white people who supported Trump, believing that their whiteness connected them, held them in common, believing in a vicarious access to his ethos/wealth/power, were in the end only an accessory to power, and realizing this, they resorted to intense white power as the only thing they could mobilize.

originates in the Black body. I like the term *Black*, capital B, because it points to how Black people are unified by our loss of heritage, the unknowability of our lineage in all details, unlike white people, whose category breaks down into German, Scottish, French, etc.
I like the term *racialized* too, because it shows that race has been enacted upon people. There is a full, living person beneath racialization.

"god term." Here's Richard M. Weaver's definition: "By 'god term' we mean that expression about which all other expressions are ranked as subordinate and serving dominations and powers. Its force imparts to the others their lesser degree of force, and fixes the scale by which degrees of comparison are understood." *The Ethics of Rhetoric* (Davis, CA: Hermagoras Press, 1953), 212.

Consider the price of kidneys. The costs are from around 2003. Nancy Scheper-Hughes, "Keeping an Eye on the Global Traffic in Human Organs," *Lancet* 361.9369 (2003): 1645–48, doi.org/10.1016/S0140-6736(03)13305-3. Check out the Organs Watch Project.

price of a Black slave. Samuel H. Williamson and Louis P. Cain estimate that "the 'real price' of $400 in 1850 [average price of a slave then] would be approximately $12,000 in 2016 prices." Samuel H. Williamson and Louis Cain, "Measuring Slavery in 2016 Dollars," MeasuringWorth.com, 2021, measuringworth.com/slavery.php.

not the domain of a single race. "Who is the Tolstoy of the Zulus?" Ta-Nehisi Coates quotes Saul Bellow. The answer: "'Tolstoy is the Tolstoy of the Zulus,' wrote [Ralph] Wiley. 'Unless you find a profit in fencing off universal properties of mankind into exclusive tribal ownership.'" Ta-Nehisi Coates, *Between the World and Me* (New York: Spiegel & Grau, 2015), 43, 56.

capitalism requires inequities to thrive. See Eric Williams's landmark examination, *Capitalism and Slavery* (1944).

over eight hundred military bases in foreign countries. According to David Vine writing in *Politico Magazine* in 2015 ("Where in the World Is the US Military?"):
Despite recently closing hundreds of bases in Iraq and Afghanistan, the United States still maintains nearly 800 military bases in more than 70 countries and territories abroad—from giant "Little Americas" to small radar facilities. Britain, France and Russia, by contrast, have about 30 foreign bases combined. politico.com/magazine/story/2015/06/us-military-bases-around-the-world-119321#:~:text=Despite%20recently%20closing%20hundreds%20of,about%2030%20foreign%20bases%20combined.

the white, male body as the unit of humanity. Things are changing, but in 1992 Rebecca Dresser was still asking, "How did white males come to be the prototype of the human research subject?" There is a difference between *prototype* and *experimental site*; unethical studies were conducted on the Black body. Rebecca Dresser, "Wanted Single, White Male for Medical Research," *Hastings Center Report* 22.1 (1992): 24–29, doi.org/10.2307/3562720.

Jacobs's autobiography. Harriet Jacobs, *Incidents in the Life of a Slave Girl* (1861), Project Gutenberg, gutenberg.org/1/1/0/3/11030/.

whiteness relies on Blackness to understand itself. James Baldwin writes about the interaction between Blacks and whites as foundational to the American identity in *The Fire Next Time.*

We buy ourselves as white people. In the interest of efficiency, here's an optional restatement of the formerly unstated thesis, using all keywords: Whiteness exists by centring and (over)valuing itself. At all costs, it preserves itself by being adaptable, even if contradictory. It oppresses others with its power and gains power from its oppression. It finds these postulations insulting, coming from a Black person.

Four to Eighteen Days

bright sweaters tied around their necks. Ta-Nehisi Coates, *Between the World and Me* (New York: Spiegel & Grau, 2015), 127.

guess which profile attracted more responses. You can read the story and see photos in this Lifestyle article on the CTV News website (March 8, 2017): "Black Woman, 'White' Profile: Exposing Racism in Online Dating," ctvnews.ca/lifestyle/black-woman-white-profile-exposing-racism-in-online-dating-1.3315826.

People rank moving as the most stressful life event. These worst-fear surveys are everywhere. For one example, see SWNS, "Many Claim This Event Is More Stressful than Divorce or Having Kids," *New York Post*, September 30, 2020, nypost.com/2020/09/30/some-people-claim-this-is-more-stressful-than-marriage-divorce-and-even-having-kids/#:~:text=Next%20in%20line%20for%20life's,things%20they've%20ever%20experienced.

Between Us

90 percent of people who marry do so within their race. According to Pew Research, "In 2015, that number [of all interracial marriages] stood at 11 million—10% of all married people." Gretchen Livingston and Anna Brown, "Trends and Patterns in Intermarriage," Pew Research Center, Social and Demographic Trends, May 18, 2017, pewsocialtrends.org/2017/05/18/1-trends-and-patterns-in-intermarriage/#fn-22844-4.

Only 26 percent of Black women are married. These numbers are from the 2016 US census. The article "Black Marriage in America" on the Black Demographics website includes the one I cited among other interesting stats. blackdemographics.com/households/marriage-in-black-america/

The Multiculturalism Act. You can read the 1988 Government of Canada document online at laws-lois.justice.gc.ca/eng/acts/c-18.7/page-1.html.

By the most recent census numbers. "National Household Survey (NHS) Profile, 2016," www12.statcan.gc.ca/census-recensement/2016/dp-pd/index-eng.cfm.

Headlines. Tyler Stiem, "Race and Real Estate: How Hot Chinese Money Is Making Vancouver Unlivable," *Guardian*, July 7, 2016, theguardian.com/cities/2016/jul/07/vancouver-chinese-city-racism-meets-real-estate-british-columbia.

Headlines. Douglas Todd, "Immigration Has 'Undoubtedly' Escalated Housing Prices in Vancouver, Toronto, Says Study," *Vancouver Sun*, December 27, 2017, vancouversun.com/opinion/columnists/douglas-todd-canadas-immigration-targets-a-form-of-housing-policy-says-study.

Headlines. Jackie Northam, "Vancouver Has Been Transformed by Chinese Immigrants," *All Things Considered*, NPR, June 5, 2019, npr.org/2019/06/05/726531803/vancouver-has-been-transformed-by-chinese-immigrants.

Headlines. Douglas Todd, "Does China's Money Threaten Canada's Sovereignty?" *Vancouver Sun*, August 1, 2017, vancouversun.com/opinion/columnists/douglas-todd-does-chinas-money-threaten-canadas-sovereignty.

Headlines. Paul Roberts, "Is Your City Being Sold Off to Global Elites?" *Mother Jones*, May/June 2017, motherjones.com/politics /2017/05/hedge-city-vancouver-chinese-foreign-capital/.

you'll find large Chinese populations in Burnaby and Richmond. "Census Profile, 2016 Census Vancouver [Census metropolitan area], British Columbia and British Columbia [Province] Ethnic Origin," *Statistics Canada*; and "Profile of Ethnic Origin and Visible Minorities for Census Metropolitan Areas and Census Agglomerations, 2006 Census," archived October 30, 2013, at the Wayback Machine. The demographic information of both cities is summarized on Wikipedia: en.wikipedia.org/wiki/Demographics_of_Metro_Vancouver.

profitable malls. "2 of Canada's Top 3 Most Profitable Malls Are in Vancouver," *Daily Hive Vancouver*, January 15, 2019, dailyhive.com/vancouver/most-profitable-malls-vancouver-2019.

Again, of course, there are Asians in Vancouver for whom none of this is true. Definitely in the U.S., wealth disparity among Asians is greater than among other races. The Pew Research Center reports that "Asians displaced blacks as the most economically divided racial or ethnic group in the U.S." More precisely, "In 2016, Asians at the 90th percentile of their income distribution had 10.7 times the income of Asians at the 10th percentile. The 90/10 ratio among Asians was notably greater than the ratio among blacks (9.8), whites (7.8) and Hispanics (7.8)." https://www.pewresearch.org/social-trends/2018/07/12/income-inequality-in-the-u-s-is-rising-most-rapidly-among-asians/

The private education industry in Korea. According to a Korean survey, "72.8 percent of elementary, middle and high school students were receiving private education last year." The valuations of the private education industry are from 2019. See Kim Jae-heun, "Private Education Cost Reaches Record High," *Korea Times*, March 12, 2019, koreatimes.co.kr/www/nation/2020/03/181_265235.html.

routinely rated lower on such evaluations. Kerry Chávez and Kristina M.W. Mitchell, "Exploring Bias in Student Evaluations: Gender, Race, and Ethnicity," *PS: Political Science & Politics* 53.2 (April 2020): 270–74, doi.org/10.1017/S1049096519001744.

The Only

to see and also be seen by "lusty folk." The original language in Middle English is: "for to se, and eek for to be seye." Geoffrey Chaucer, "The Wife of Bath Prologue," *The Canterbury Tales*, line 552.

the act of seeing involved emitting a ray from your eye. You can get an overview of the history of optics on Wikipedia. en.wikipedia.org/wiki/Optics#Classical_optics.

degrees of concern. Here's Claudia Rankine's preferred term: "I told the students I preferred internalized dominance [to *white privilege*, i.e., Robin DiAngelo's term]. Robin DiAngelo states, 'for the dominant group being socialized to see the minority group as inferior, it conveys the dominant group is superior. The sense of superiority is often not explicit but internalized deep beneath the surface. The process causes members of the dominant group to see themselves as normal, correct, and more valuable, thus more entitled to the resources of society.'" Claudia Rankine's talk "On Whiteness," Arts Emerson, Boston, March 24, 2017, youtube.com/watch?v=uCEfUMesedE (36:07 onward).

there were two Black tables in the corner of the cafeteria. See Beverly Daniel Tatum, *Why Are All the Black Kids Sitting Together in the Cafeteria? A Psychologist Explains the Development of Racial Identity* (New York: Basic Books, 1997).

"Du Bois believes the Talented Tenth." W.E.B. Du Bois in *The Negro Problem*, Project Gutenberg, gutenberg.org/1/5/0/4/15041.

Being the Only is often reflected back to you as if it were a privilege. From the earliest times of integration, the narrative of Black people in schools is shaped as an achievement. I think of Dorothy Counts, the fifteen-year-old girl integrating into high school while being heckled by her white classmates. In a situation like that, the only thing one wants, I think, is company.

Earlier, I mentioned the scholar Christina Sharpe. See *In the Wake: On Being and Blackness* (Durham, NC: Duke University Press, 2016).

to see if Black people were, in fact, as rare as I recall. For a different take on the graph, here are the numbers of Black kids to non-Black kids in my classes:
Grade 6: no data, couldn't afford a yearbook
Grade 7: 2 of 18
Grade 8: 1 of 20
Grade 9: couldn't afford a yearbook
Grade 10: 8 of 374
Grade 11: 5 of 333
Grade 12: 8 of 333
Graduating class at university: 8 of 397

Certain kinds of trauma. Toni Morrison's MLA talk was later published. Toni Morrison, "Guest Column: Roundtable on the Future of the Humanities in a Fragmented World," *PMLA* 120.3 (2005): 717.

The question of "speaking" as. Gayatri Chakravorty Spivak, "Questions of Multiculturalism," interview with Sneja Gunew, *The Cultural Studies Reader*, ed. Simon During (Abingdon, UK: Routledge, 1993), 195.

"The white man takes the astonishment as tribute." James Baldwin, *Notes of a Native Son* (Boston: Beacon Press, 2012), 168.

The Drive Home

police in Colorado drew their guns. Oliver Milman, "Police Draw Guns on Black Woman and Children in Mistaken Stolen Car Stop," *Guardian*, August 4, 2020, theguardian.com/us-news/2020/aug/04/colorado-police-draw-guns-mistaken-stolen-car-stop-video-black-woman-brittney-gilliam.

"Can you prove that you bought this car?" "Danny Rose Reveals

Racist Treatment in Everyday Life," Skysports.com, August 3, 2020, skysports.com/football/news/11095/12041656/danny-rose-reveals-racist-treatment-in-everyday-life.

Two Eyes, a Nose, and a Mouth

"and he needs you to account for that." Claudia Rankine, *Citizen* (Minneapolis, MN: Graywolf Press, 2014), 46.

"respiratory depression." Richard J. Levy, "Clinical Effects and Lethal and Forensic Aspects of Propofol," *Journal of Forensic Sciences* 56.1 (January 2011): S142–47, doi.org/10.1111/j.1556-4029.2010.01583.x.

"airway obstruction." Joanne M. Goralka, "Propofol," chap. 226 in *Poisoning & Drug Overdose* (New York: McGraw-Hill, 2012).

"read the autopsy report." The person who posted goes by pat4merica.instagram.com/p/CCpepLGnLN0/?igshid=najuy2bpkasm.

"Nobody says nothing about that." You can watch a clip of Oprah's interview with Michael Jackson on YouTube, youtube.com/watch?v=w20H0L555cE.

"Yeah, but so did a lot of people that I know." Listen around 27:30 of the Oprah interview, youtube.com/watch?v=CqxAL4L-3bg.

"without loss of their ethnic identity" and *Black patients ask for reduced width.* Adeyiza O. Momoh et al., "Rhinoplasty: The African American Patient," *Seminars in Plastic Surgery* 23.3 (2009): 223–31, doi.org/10.1055/s-0029-1224802.

universal features of humans. I realize the ableist normativity at work in the positioning of this chapter. Not everyone has two eyes, a nose, and a mouth that work optimally.

Lil' Kim posted photos to her Instagram. The original post of Lil' Kim's transformation has since been removed by Lil' Kim, but remnants are everywhere. See Victoria Anderson, "Lil' Kim and the Unbearable Whiteness of Being," *The Conversation*, April 28, 2016, theconversation.com/lil-kim-and-the-unbearable-whiteness-of-being-58459.

"When it comes to Black people." Treasure also says, "I act and think like a white person."
Video: "'When It Comes to Black People, I Think They're All Ugly,' Says 16-Year-Old African-American," Dr. Phil YouTube channel, posted October 24, 2018, youtube.com/watch?time_continue=3&v=2TPFBI2sYik&feature=emb_logo.
Article: Yesha Callahan, "16-Year-Old Black Teen Tells Dr. Phil She's White and Hates Black People," *Essence*, October 25, 2018, essence.com/news/16-year-old-black-teen-tells-dr-phil-shes-white-and-hates-black-people/.

direction of these transracial desires. Incidentally, I don't mean to conflate transgender movements with transracial thought. Totally separate.

"It's a unique kind of beauty" and other quotations. Leon Talley's comments are part of a segment on Alek Wek produced by FashionTV: "Alek Wek: Controversial Modeling Debut," YouTube video posted August 31, 2013, youtube.com/watch?v=envPStPNPXI&feature=youtu.be.

Cladisticizing. The term is Wayde Compton's. See *After Canaan* (Vancouver: Arsenal Pulp Press, 2010), 25.

There is no deception on their part. Pheneticized is the term Wayde Compton uses to put the fault of the error on the viewer. See Ibid., 23–24.

ACKNOWLEDGEMENTS

Excerpts of "Disorientation" appeared in *Granta*; "The Drive Home" in *The Globe and Mail*; "Two Eyes, a Nose, and a Mouth" in *The Kenyon Review*; "More than Half of Americans Can't Swim" was delivered as the Pelham Edgar Lecture at Victoria College, University of Toronto, and an excerpt published in *Publishers Weekly*; "Four to Eighteen Days" was part of the Toronto International Festival of Authors' Skin Hunger project. Thank you to the editors and programmers: Josie Mitchell, Mark Medley, Nicole Terez Dutton, Angela Esterhammer, Edward Nawotka, Brianna Cooze.

This book is possible thanks to:

My agent, Denise Bukowski, who knew I would write this book before I did. And thank you, Stacy Small.

Anne Collins at Random House Canada. This was not an easy book to edit. You were not afraid of it. Thank you,

Scott Sellers, for connecting this book and *Reproduction* to readers. Thanks also to others at Random House: Sarah Jackson, Lisa Jager, Deirdre Molina, and John Sweet.

Three Black guys, so different from each other, but all brilliant: Phanuel Antwi, Jean Claude, Myronn Hardy.

The Vancouver Friday crew: Tariq Hussain, Emily Pohl-Weary, Rhea Tregebov, Doretta Lau, Suzanne Andrew, Kevin Chong, Paolo Pietropaulo.

The people who appeared with food when I wasn't leaving the house: Aaron Rabinowitz for the cobblers, Paul Dhillon for the lasagne and curries. Thank you, Jane Munro, Justin Morris, Maria Melititskaya, Aaron Sikhosana.

The tennis crew: Ted Slingerland, Dave Handler, Ben Cutler.

The three people with whom I share a family name.

Moon who is always there.

Chiayi who is always here.